The spiritual awakening of a chosen one

©2024 BossesMadeMen. ISBN **9798324571269**
The year of publication of the book. No part of this publication may be reproduced, distributed, or transmitted in any form or by any means, including photocopying, recording, or other electronic or mechanical methods, without the prior written permission of the publisher, except in the case of brief quotations embodied in critical reviews

Spiritual Awakening 147

Table of Contents

Table of Contents

Introduction..3
Chapter 1: The Spiritual Battlefield.................6
Chapter 2: Spiritual Warfare in the Streets.....21
Chapter 3: A Testimony of Divine Protection 33
Chapter 4: Declaring the Glory of God..........62
Chapter 5: Reclaiming the Hebrew Heritage. 76
Chapter 6: Walking in the Spirit.....................93
Chapter 7: Power of Words and the Tongue...99
Chapter 8: The Armor of God......................104
Chapter 9: Living as a Chosen People.........109
Chapter 10: The Journey of Endurance........119
Chapter 11: Spiritual Warfare Prayers..........130
Chapter 12: Praise and Declaring God's Glory
....138
    Notes for Readers................................149
    Additional Resources for Spiritual Growth and Understanding.................149
    Suggestions for Further Reading........150
    Acknowledgments..............................152
        About the Author............................154

Spiritual Awakening 147

Introduction

In a time of spiritual confusion and deep divisions, where the search for truth often leads through winding and uncertain paths, we find ourselves reaching for a guiding light. "The Book of James: The Called and Chosen" aims to be that beacon, casting a hopeful glow into the darkness of doubt and uncertainty.

Brother James, a dedicated minister and leader of the Spiritual Awakening Project 147, has long been a steadfast voice for unity and reconciliation among believers. In this autobiography, he takes us through his personal journey—a journey that transcends boundaries, connecting believers from all walks of life, Jew and Gentile alike, through the universal message of salvation in Christ.

As the editor of this testament to faith and spiritual awakening, I have witnessed first-hand the power of Brother James's words. His teachings offer more than simple guidance; they invite us to embrace a deeper understanding of ourselves and our place in the divine plan. This project, born of a collaboration between the Spiritual Awakening Project 147 and the Love God Now initiative, is designed to bridge the gaps that often divide

Spiritual Awakening 147

us. It seeks to create a platform where individuals of various spiritual beliefs can come together, united by a shared yearning for spiritual truth and enlightenment.

Through this series, we explore the diverse teachings and ideological challenges that both test and strengthen our faith. Brother James invites us to reflect on the Scriptures, encouraging a dialogue that transcends the rigid confines of traditional religious dogma. It is his mission, and ours, to open doors for those who seek solace and understanding in the Word of Yah Almighty.

This book is not merely an account of Brother James's life; it is a roadmap for those who yearn to connect with the divine. It is filled with testimonies of transformation, stories of hope, and a profound call to embrace the love and salvation offered by our Lord, Christ Yahshua. As we delve into these pages, may we find inspiration to carry on our own spiritual journeys, united in faith and guided by the eternal light of God's grace.

It is with great reverence and a humble heart that I, John Livingston, dedicate this work to all seekers of truth and believers in the power of spiritual awakening 147. May it touch your

Spiritual Awakening 147

soul and guide you to the revelation and beauty that lie within the gospel's teachings. Together, let us embark on this journey, ready to embrace the challenges and the glory that await.

James Stephenson - Servant of God - The Healer - In His service - Spiritual Awakening 147

In His Service,
John Livingston – The Messenger

Spiritual Awakening 147

Chapter 1: The Spiritual Battlefield

It was a night like any other—quiet, still, and drawing you inward. In the dim light of my modest study, I sat in deep contemplation, my Bible open to the familiar pages of scripture. It was in this moment of reflection that the call came, clear and undeniable, like a whisper in the wind that cuts through the silence.

The voice on the other end belonged to Brother James, a man of God and a fellow seeker of truth. His tone was urgent as I was reading Ephesians 6:10-18, the passage about the whole armour of God. "Finally, be strong in the Lord and in His mighty power he said Put on the full armor of God, so that you can take your stand against the devil's schemes." We exchanged greetings, but it wasn't long before the conversation turned serious. I assured him that we'd handle the situation with grace and understanding, recognizing that we're all seekers on different journeys. As we talked, we glanced back at the Bible, where **Ephesians 6:12** reminded us that "our struggle is not against flesh and blood, but against the rulers, against the authorities, against the powers of this dark world, and against the spiritual forces of evil in the heavenly realms." This verse seemed particularly relevant to our conversation about the ideological divides that often separate Christians and Muslims.

We discussed the story of Ishmael, the son of Abraham, whose lineage led to a different understanding of the same stories we knew from the Bible. In the Arabic tradition, the name of the prophet is Isa, not Yahshua or Yeshua, James spoke and added the path to salvation follows a different course. Despite these differences, we agreed that respect and understanding were crucial in bridging the gaps that divide us.

Our discussion reminded me of **Romans 14:19,** which says, "Let us therefore make every effort to do what leads to peace and to mutual edification." It was a powerful call to focus on what unites us rather than what divides us. As Brother James and I continued to talk, we found common ground in our shared desire to seek spiritual truth and to serve the Most High.

Spiritual Awakening 147

8

In His Service,

James – The servant of the MOST HIGH YAH

The man of God responded with fervour, testifying that YAH saved him through the resurrection of Yahshua. "It's an essential part of our faith," he said. I nodded, agreeing that it is through faith that we find understanding, as he referencing **Romans 10:17:** "Faith comes from hearing, and hearing through the word of Christ."

Brother James then explained his belief that all people, including Christians, had once called upon YAH, even if they did not yet have the full revelation of the Son. It was an intriguing notion, one that spoke to the universality of the human search for the divine. "How do you feel about that?" I asked, curious about Brother James's perspective.

Yet, through mutual respect and meaningful conversation, there was hope for building bridges. As Ministers, it's important to approach these topics with sensitivity, ensuring that the text respects different beliefs while promoting unity.

9

The call that night wasn't just a simple conversation; it was a reminder that spiritual journeys are about constant growth and learning. The key was to maintain open hearts and minds to find common ground, even amid profound differences. As we continued to discuss and share, I felt a greater sense of purpose—a call to serve and bring together those who seek the truth, no matter where they are on their journey.

Minister James and I talked about the significance of spiritual awakening and the role of the Holy Spirit in bringing people to a revelation of Christ. He referred to **1 Corinthians 12:3**, where Paul states:

"Therefore I want you to understand that no one speaking by the Spirit of God ever says 'Yahshua is accursed!' and no one can say 'Yahshua is Lord' except by the Holy Spirit." This verse highlighted that recognizing Yahshua as Lord is a spiritual revelation, a bridge connecting believers across different backgrounds.

As we reflect on these conversations, we understand the importance of legalities and editing principles. For Ministers, ensuring accurate representation of religious texts and avoiding infringement of copyright is crucial. Proper citation and referencing are essential to maintain the book's credibility and avoid legal issues. It's also important to avoid statements that could be seen as defamatory or disrespectful to other faiths.

This chapter demonstrates the ongoing journey of spiritual exploration and growth. It underlines the importance of approaching religious dialogues with a spirit of reconciliation and unity. As ministers, our role is to ensure that the narrative fosters understanding, aligns with legal requirements, and supports the overarching message of faith and spiritual awakening.

Our conversation shifted to the historical timeline of the scriptures. Minister James pointed out that the Bible was established at least six hundred years before the Quran, providing an overview of the historical context and how the sacred texts came to be. This was an enlightening moment, a reminder of the complex layers of religious history that have influenced our faiths.

"Glory to the Most High God!"

11

Minister James nodded, his expression filled with compassion and concern. "It burdens my soul," he said, "that some of our brothers miss this vital point about the revelation of Christ. It's almost offensive to suggest otherwise, but I'm doing my best to reach these souls and gather them to Christ." The ideological and theological divides were real, and they created barriers that were not easily overcome. Yet the Spirit urged us to persist, to keep reaching out despite the obstacles.

Spiritual Awakening 147

12

As Minister James spoke, I took notes, capturing his words as the Spirit guided our conversation. The story of Thomas, with his initial doubt and eventual belief, became a symbol of hope—proof that even those who struggle with faith can find their way to Christ through the power of the Holy Spirit.

I thanked Minister James for his time and wisdom, praising the God of Heaven for the revelations that had come to us during this conversation. It was clear that our calling was more than a personal journey—it was a mission to build bridges, foster understanding, and bring the light of Christ to those in need. As I closed my notes, I felt a renewed sense of purpose, ready to continue this journey and share the message of salvation with a world in need of healing and unity.

As our conversation deepened, Minister James shared some of the challenges we face when it comes to discerning truth from erroneous doctrines. "It's not just about one religion," he said, with a hint of sorrow in his voice. "There are people across all beliefs who lead others astray. It's easy to get caught up in teachings that sound right but don't align with the Word of God." He paused, reflecting on the seriousness of this truth, then added, "We're all sinners; we need to repent daily and stay rooted in the Holy Spirit."

His words were a reminder that spiritual growth requires constant vigilance and a commitment to the truth. As we navigate the complexities of spiritual warfare, it's essential to keep our focus on God, to stay rooted in the scriptures, and to rely on the Holy Spirit for discernment. The journey is long and often difficult, but with faith and determination, we can overcome any obstacle and walk in the light of Christ.

God's grace and mercy are present in the stones we use to build our faith," James said, referencing **1 Peter 2:5: "You also, like living stones, are being built into a spiritual house to be a holy priesthood, offering spiritual sacrifices acceptable to God through Yahshua Christ."**

"The Spirit works through us," he continued, "guiding us as we build the body of Christ. Sometimes the earliest stages of planting a vision looks like chaos, but that's where the good seeds grow."

He nodded, a glimmer of hope returning to his eyes. We began to talk about the mysterious ways God works, how He places people and circumstances in our paths to guide us, even when we can't see the bigger picture. It was a moment of agreement, a reminder that the journey of faith is rarely straightforward, but God's provision is always there, even in the midst of uncertainty. As **Isaiah 55:8-9 reminds us, "For my thoughts are not your thoughts, neither are your ways my ways," declares the Lord. "As the heavens are higher than the earth, so are my ways higher than your ways and my thoughts than your thoughts."**

We glorified the Father together, acknowledging His hand in our lives, His ability to use us as vessels for His work. It was a powerful realization that the call to ministry isn't about finding a specific church or location; it's about being open to the Spirit's leading, wherever it may take us. Brother James's journey was unique, but it resonated with my own experiences, the times when I felt lost but found comfort in God's mysterious provision.

As our conversation drew to a close, I felt a renewed sense of purpose. The call to serve isn't confined to a single place or building; it's a way of life, a commitment to follow wherever God leads. And as long as we stay

15

rooted in the Spirit and seek His guidance, we will find our way. Brother James and I parted ways that night, but I knew our paths would cross again. The journey of faith is a shared experience, and we were both walking the same road, seeking the same truth.

He told me that this book would also be an appeal to those stones to join him in the mission for Christ, in spreading the gospel and bringing others—even from different folds—to share their testimonials and faith in God through scripture." The words of Brother James echoed in my heart as I listened to his vision for this new work. It wasn't just about telling his story; it was about inviting others to be part of a larger mission, a mission to unite believers in the truth of God's Word.

In this new mission, Brother James seeks to bridge gaps between faiths and bring unity among believers. As Romans 10:12-13 reminds us, "For there is no distinction between Jew and Greek; for the same Lord is Lord of all, bestowing His riches on all who call on Him. For 'everyone who calls on the name of the Lord will be saved.'" This broader vision was not just about one person's journey, but about the collective journey of faith, inviting everyone to be part of the larger story that God is writing.

I applauded the Man of Yah for his vision. "Press on," I encouraged him. "Your calling is a great one, and I would be privileged to help write what you've experienced and learned along the way." We discussed the logistics of the book—the structure and flow—and some of the key points he wanted to include. These included stories of trials and tribulations, dark moments and moments of revelation, and times when he felt lost and then found by the grace of God.

Throughout our discussion, Brother James shared his experiences with raw honesty, which I found deeply inspiring. It was clear that his journey had not been easy, but every step of the way had been guided by a higher power. As we spoke, we both felt the presence of the Spirit, a reminder that even in our trials, God is always with us, leading us toward His purposes. In **Isaiah 41:10,** we are reminded, "Fear not, for I am with you; be not dismayed, for I am your God; I will strengthen you, I will help you, I will uphold you with my righteous right hand."

"Glory be to the Most High Yah,"

17

I thanked minister James Feeling the warmth of divine reassurance in my soul. "Your story is a testament to the power of faith, to the way God takes our broken pieces and makes something beautiful." My words seemed inadequate to express the depth of my gratitude for this moment, but they were the best I could find.

Brother James smiled, his eyes filled with determination. He knew that the journey ahead would be challenging, but he was ready to embrace it. "It's not just about me," he said. "It's about all of us. We're all part of this greater story, and my hope is that this book will inspire others to find their place in God's plan."

As we concluded our conversation, I felt a renewed sense of purpose, not just for this book, but for the journey ahead. The work of the gospel is never done, and each of us has a role to play in spreading the good news. Brother James had found his calling, We are reminded in **Matthew 28:19-20** that the Great Commission is a collective mission: "Go therefore and make disciples of all nations, baptizing them in the name of the Father and of the Son and of the Holy Spirit, teaching them to observe all that I have commanded you. And

Spiritual Awakening

18

behold, I am with you always, to the end of the age."

As we prayed, our voices blended in harmony as we thanked the Saviour for bringing us through the most trying of times. The Spirit's presence was tangible, a warmth that seemed to light up the room. Brother James and I testified to the ways in which the Lord had saved us—saved us from drugs, from guns, from prison, from sickness, from witches and warlocks, and all manner of evil and darkness. It was a profound moment of unity, a testament to the power of prayer and the enduring presence of God. It was a testimony to God's boundless grace and mercy, a reminder that even in our darkest moments, He is there to lift us out of the shadows. **Psalm 23:4** resonates with this sentiment: **"Even though I walk through the valley of the shadow of death, I will fear no evil, for You are with me; Your rod and Your staff, they comfort me."**

We prayed together, asking for God's guidance and blessing on the project. **Psalms 119:105 encapsulates this sense of guidance: "Your word is a lamp to my feet and a light to my path."**

Spiritual Awakening 147

When the prayer concluded, I felt compelled to ask Brother James about his own journey, about the moment he received the revelation of Christ. "Brother, would you share with me your testimony?" I asked, sensing that his story held deep significance.

"The Lord spoke to me, brother," he said, his voice rising with excitement, "and He told me things personally. The Lord told me to stay on the path I was on."

The Apostle Paul reminds us in **Philippians 4:6-7 "Do not be anxious about anything, but in everything by prayer and supplication with thanksgiving, let your requests be made known to God. And the peace of God, which surpasses all understanding, will guard your hearts and minds in Christ Yahshua."**

"May the Lord guide you, And may He bring clarity to your path." This echoed the words of Proverbs 3:5-6, where we are reminded to trust in the Lord with all our hearts: **"Trust in the Lord with all your heart, and do not lean on your own understanding. In all your ways acknowledge Him, and He will make straight your paths."**

Spiritual Awakening 147

"Glory to the Most High Yah," he continued, his voice filled with a sense of purpose and had a prophetic preacher tone.

I knew that the journey ahead would be filled with both challenges and blessings. But with God's guidance and the strength of the Spirit, I was confident that my story would touch many hearts and lead others to the truth of the gospel he continued the call had been made, and now it was time to answer. **Romans 10:13** reminds us of the simplicity of salvation: **"For everyone who calls on the name of the Lord will be saved."**

Brother James share his testimony, bringing light and hope to a world in need.

Chapter 2: Spiritual Warfare in the Streets

The silence between us was filled with the hum of the evening. I felt the weight of Brother James's words, his testimony leaving me in deep thought. There was more to his story, I knew that, but he was right—this wasn't the time to delve into every detail. Yet the brief glimpse he gave into the spiritual battles he had faced was enough to remind me of the realities we often try to ignore. Brother James mentioned that the Lord had revealed to him who was working against him with dark arts. It was a powerful moment, a reminder that even in the midst of darkness, the light of God remains steadfast. In **John 1:5, it says, "The light shines in the darkness, and the darkness has not overcome it."** This scripture echoed the sentiment of our conversation, highlighting that no matter how intense the spiritual warfare, God's light cannot be extinguished. Brother James continued, explaining the playing field on which we, the children of God, find ourselves. "It's a spiritual

22

war," he said, "between the children of God and the children of the devil." His words were a stark reminder of truth weighed heavily on the heart. Despite the constant threats from those who operate in shadows, Brother James stood firm. "Yet I am still here by His grace," he said with a sense of victory in his voice. It reminded us of **2 Corinthians 12:9,** where the Lord tells Paul, **"My grace is sufficient for you, for my power is made perfect in weakness."** Brother James's resilience and faith, despite the spiritual warfare he had faced, were living proof of this divine grace. As he shared his experiences, I felt a mix of awe and respect for his journey. The spiritual battles he described were real and daunting, yet he remained undeterred, his faith unshaken. "The enemy will try to break you," he said, "but we have the armour of God, and we stand on the rock of salvation." This was a reference to **Ephesians 6:13-17,** where Paul describes the full armour of God: the belt of truth, the breastplate of righteousness, the shield of faith, the helmet of salvation, and the sword of the Spirit. As our conversation deepened resonating with many. His journey was a

23

testament to the strength of faith, even when faced with the darkest of adversaries. The spiritual warfare in the streets was relentless, but so was God's power and protection. With this realization, highlighted the ongoing spiritual war between good and evil and the unwavering faith required to navigate it. It was a reminder that even in the streets, where darkness often prevails, the children of God stand strong

The silence between us was filled with the hum of the evening. I felt the weight of Brother James's words, his testimony leaving me in deep thought. There was more to his story, I knew that, but he was right—this wasn't the time to delve into every detail. Yet the brief glimpse he gave into the spiritual battles he had faced was enough to remind me of the realities we often try to ignore. Brother James mentioned that the Lord had revealed to him who was working against him with dark arts. It was a powerful moment, a reminder that even in the midst of darkness, the light of God remains steadfast. In **John 1:5**, it says, "The light shines in the darkness, and the darkness has not overcome it." This scripture echoed the

Spiritual Awakening 147

sentiment of our conversation, highlighting that no matter how intense the spiritual warfare, God's light cannot be extinguished. Brother James continued, explaining the playing field on which we, the children of God, find ourselves. "It's a spiritual war," he said, "between the children of God and the children of the devil." His words were a stark reminder of **Ephesians 6:12, which states, "For our struggle is not against flesh and blood, but against the rulers, against the authorities, against the powers of this dark world, and against the spiritual forces of evil in the heavenly realms.**" This truth weighed heavily on my heart. Despite the constant threats from those who operate in shadows, Brother James stood firm. "Yet I am still here by His grace," he said with a sense of victory in his voice. It reminded me of **2 Corinthians 12:9,** where the Lord tells Paul, **"My grace is sufficient for you, for my power is made perfect in weakness."** Brother James's resilience and faith, despite the spiritual warfare he had faced, were living proof of this divine grace. As he shared his experiences, I felt a mix of awe and respect for his journey. The spiritual battles he described were real and daunting, yet he remained undeterred, his faith unshaken. "The enemy will try to break you," he said, "but we have the armour of God, and we stand on the rock of salvation." This was a reference to **Ephesians 6:13-17,** where Paul describes the full armour of God: the belt of truth, the breastplate of righteousness, the shield of faith, the helmet of salvation, and the sword of the Spirit. As our conversation concluded, I knew that the story of Brother James would resonate with many. His journey was a testament to the strength of faith, even when faced with the darkest of adversaries. The spiritual warfare in the streets was relentless, but so was God's power and protection. The battle continues, but so does the victory in Christ. With this assurance, we press on, knowing that the final outcome has already been decided in our favour

"It's a tragedy," Brother James said, his voice carrying a mix of anger and sorrow. "The children of the devil—what they do, their works are abominable. They strive to destroy us, brother." His conviction was unmistakable, the urgency in his words a reflection of the

26

spiritual battles we all face. The moral decay, the rise of violence, and the breakdown of families were signs of a deeper spiritual malaise. It was 2024, and the world seemed more chaotic than ever. Crime was rising, and traditional values were being eroded. People were losing hope, turning to whatever could offer a momentary escape from reality. In **Romans 1:28-32, Paul describes a society that has turned away from God, resulting in a culture filled with unrighteousness, wickedness, and disobedience.**

God's light is always present, guiding us through the chaos. "We must remain vigilant," he said, echoing **1 Peter 5:8: "Be alert and of sober mind. Your enemy the devil prowls around like a roaring lion, looking for someone to devour."**

The spiritual battle was intense, but so was our resolve to fight for the truth. There was much work to be done, and I was ready to stand with Brother James and others who were committed to spiritual warfare. It was a battle worth fighting, for the stakes were high, but the

27

victory in Christ was assured. As I reflected on our conversation, I knew that our mission was clear: to stand firm, to remain faithful, and to trust in God's ultimate plan. The road ahead was daunting, but it was clear that this battle wasn't ours alone. We were not just fighting against flesh and blood but against "the rulers, against the authorities, against the cosmic powers over this present darkness, against the spiritual forces of evil in the heavenly places" **(Ephesians 6:12). And for that, we needed the full armor of God.**

It wasn't just about telling a story — it was about awakening people to the spiritual realities we face and reminding them that in Christ, we have already won the ultimate victory. The next chapter will take us deeper into this spiritual awakening, and I was ready to confront whatever came our way, with God's guidance and protection.

"Sometimes the Lord has to separate us for us to hear from Him and minimize the distractions," James the healer continued, his voice firm but filled with compassion. As his story unfolded, I felt the truth in his words. Separation, though painful, could be a divine intervention to help us realign our focus recalling a time when the Spirit told James to move to a place where he knew no one, a place that was far removed from the life He knew.

The calling was clear, but the path was uncertain. "I had to follow the call, and it led me to a strange place," He explained. "But it was there that I found the space I needed to focus on the Lord. It was a fresh start, and I was willing to embrace it." But the only move that matters is the move of the Holy Spirit. When the Lord calls us to separate, it's for a purpose." His words brought to mind **Matthew 10:34-36,** where Yahshua said, "Do not think that I have come to bring peace to the earth; I have not come to bring peace, but a sword. For I have come to set a man against his father, and a daughter against her mother." Separation, when guided by the Spirit, has divine purpose.

I nodded in agreement, acknowledging the complexity of this spiritual battle. "There are so many levels to it," He said. "The enemy is crafty, always finding ways to create rifts among us. But when it's the Spirit that guides us, even separation can be a blessing in disguise." This idea of spiritual separation is reflected in **2 Corinthians 6:17,** where Paul instructs believers to **"come out from among**

them and be separate," indicating that sometimes God's calling involves distancing from influences that do not align with His will.

The call to share the gospel and reveal spiritual truths is a shared responsibility, one that requires courage and faith. With God as our guide and the Holy Spirit leading the way, demonstrated the power of spiritual discernment and the importance of following the Spirit's guidance. It also highlighted the reality of spiritual warfare and the craftiness of the enemy, emphasizing the need for vigilance and discernment. With God's strength, I knew we could face any obstacle and continue to spread the message of faith, hope, and redemption.

The spiritual awakening wasn't just about recognizing the battles; it was about finding strength in the separation, knowing that sometimes the Lord's plan required us to step away from the familiar to discover a deeper connection with Him.

Brother James continued, saying that we would let the Spirit guide the direction of his story. He wasn't concerned about how the fleshly beginnings might unfold in his testimonial because the Spirit would reveal what was

30

needed. "One must always start where they are," he said, his voice carrying a sense of conviction. "That's how this story unfolds—from the ground up, letting the Spirit take us to where we need to be." "Let's use our gifts to create something that honors the Lord, and He will provide the rest." Brother James smiled, and we both shared an "Alleluia," feeling the shared sense of commitment to the work ahead.

Galatians 6:9: "Let us not become weary in doing good, for at the proper time we will reap a harvest if we do not give up." The key was to rightly divide the Word, ensuring that the spiritual awakening we hoped to share was clear and true.

Brother James added "I don't want to focus on the flesh," he said. "My story is about spiritual awakening, not just about the details of my past. It's the transformation that matters, not the circumstances that led me here." This focus on transformation aligns with **Romans 12:2, which encourages us not to conform to the pattern of this world, but to be transformed by the renewing of our minds.**

It's tempting to get caught up in the worldly aspects, but this is about something deeper. This concept is reflected in **Ephesians 4:25,**

which instructs us to "put off falsehood and speak truthfully to our neighbour."

Brother James said, shaking his head. "We must not join him." The reference to the devil being a liar is found in **John 8:44, where Yahshua describes Satan as a murderer from the beginning and the father of lies. This understanding underscores the importance of truth in our spiritual journey.**

It was a moment of levity, but it underscored the deeper truth we both knew: the journey toward spiritual awakening is about embracing truth and rejecting the lies that can so easily entangle us. The devil is always looking for ways to deceive, but as long as we remain rooted in Christ, we have the power to resist. **James 4:7** offers the key to victory: **"Submit yourselves, then, to God. Resist the devil, and he will flee from you."**

This conversation with Brother James served as a reminder that the path to spiritual growth is not just about avoiding sin but about seeking the truth and letting the Spirit guide us. The road ahead might be challenging, but with God's grace and our commitment to His truth, we can navigate it with confidence and hope.

Spiritual Awakening 147

The work would require patience and dedication, but with the Spirit's guidance, we get ready to take on the challenge. **Galatians 6:2**—which says, **"Carry each other's burdens, and in this way you will fulfil the law of Christ."** The weight of its meaning settled on me. As believers, we are called to support one another, to help each other carry the crosses we bear. Iron sharpens iron, as **Proverbs 27:17** reminds us, and in the body of Christ, we are interconnected, each one bringing unique gifts and strengths to the table.

Chapter 3: A Testimony of Divine Protection

I felt a surge of spiritual energy coursing through me, like a wave of creative guidance. The Spirit was prompting the man of God, and What's on your mind today?" He didn't hesitate. "Today, spiritual warfare," he said, his voice carrying a sense of urgency. "We are surrounded by unseen forces, and we need to be vigilant. People don't always realize the dangers of the spiritual realm. You must watch the company you keep because some are under serious possession and influenced by demonic entities." His words were a stark reminder of the ongoing battle between light and darkness.

I nodded, taking in the gravity of his message. "You're right, Brother James. The spiritual battlefield is real, and the enemy is cunning. We need to be armoured in faith and discernment to stand firm.

Spiritual Awakening 147

34

The conversation deepened as Brother James explained the various tactics the enemy uses to infiltrate our lives. "There are spirits that attack in different ways," he said. "Some are subtle, while others are outright confrontational. You must be aware of the spirit realm, because it's always active, whether we see it or not."

"True," I replied. "It's a constant battle. We need to stay close to God, praying and seeking His protection. Only then can we withstand the schemes of the enemy." This echoed 1 Peter 5:8, which advises believers to "be alert and of sober mind. Your enemy the devil prowls around like a roaring lion, looking for someone to devour." The spiritual realm is always active, and we must be prepared to resist its threats.

Brother James agreed, his voice carrying the weight of experience. "Exactly. That's why prayer and the Word are so important. They are our weapons against the forces of darkness. Without them, we are defenceless." His conviction was clear, reinforcing the importance of staying grounded in Scripture and constant communication with God. This

35

sentiment aligns with **2 Corinthians 10:4,** which reminds us that "the weapons we fight with are not the weapons of the world. On the contrary, they have divine power to demolish strongholds."

As our conversation continued, I sensed the importance of documenting Brother James's journey. His testimony was a powerful illustration of the battles we face in the spiritual realm and the victory we have in Christ. The work ahead would require patience and dedication, but with the guidance of the Holy Spirit, we were ready to face it. I knew this chapter would serve as a wake-up call, a reminder that spiritual warfare is real, but so is God's protection.

The more he spoke, the more I realized the depth of the spiritual warfare we faced. The enemy's strategies were diverse, from sowing discord to attacking our faith. Brother James mentioned that some people operate in darkness, sending spirits to disrupt and cause harm. It was a sobering thought, and I knew we needed to be vigilant. **1 Peter 5:8** reminds us, "Be alert and of sober mind. Your enemy the devil prowls around like a roaring lion, looking for someone to devour." This was no ordinary battle; it was a constant struggle against unseen forces.

"Let's reflect on this for a bit," Brother James said. "I'll call you after 8 to continue our discussion. Take some time to pray and meditate on what we've talked about." I agreed, knowing that reflection and prayer were essential to understanding the complexities of the spiritual realm. As we ended the call, I felt a sense of anticipation mixed with a bit of trepidation. The battle was real, and we needed to be prepared for whatever came our way.

That evening, at 8 PM, I set the stage with a question to spark the most beautiful narrative: "Brother James, when was the first time you had a spiritual awakening?"

He began his story. "I was sitting in the cab station in Brixton, feeling the hum of the city around me. It was a typical night—bustling, noisy, alive. But tonight felt different. There was a tension in the air, a sense of something brewing just below the surface. People were whispering, casting anxious glances over their

Spiritual Awakening 147

shoulders. I couldn't quite put my finger on it, but the energy was off."

Then he walked in. A tall man, dressed in dark clothing, his eyes filled with anger and fierce determination. He stormed past the counter, pushing his way through the crowded room. I felt my stomach tighten. This wasn't just any man—this was someone on a mission. A mission of revenge. He stopped in front of the glass screen that separated the dispatch area from the waiting room, his eyes scanning the crowd. Everyone fell silent, sensing the danger that had just entered the room.

Brother James described the fear that gripped the room, but he felt the presence of God with him, a calm amidst the storm. "It was as if a protective shield surrounded me, insulating me from the growing chaos," he said. The shop owner noticed the man's aggressive demeanour and tried hit the ground, as the man brandished a gun, his focus solely on the target he sought. Suddenly, there was a click, and that's when he realized the man had a gun.

Spiritual Awakening 147

Panic spread through the room. People ducked for cover, some diving behind chairs, others scrambling for the exit. But Brother James stayed rooted to his spot, watching as the man tried to fire his weapon. "I could see his frustration as he pulled the trigger, but nothing happened," he said. "The gun didn't fire. He pulled it again—nothing. He tried again and again, but it was as if the weapon had been rendered useless."

Psalm 91:11-12 "For He will command His angels concerning you to guard you in all your ways; they will lift you up in their hands, so that you will not strike your foot against a stone." It was a testament to divine protection, a miraculous moment where Brother James experienced the power of God intervening in a dangerous situation. As he recounted this story, I felt the significance of his journey, knowing that the spiritual warfare we face is real, but so is the Lord's protection. This chapter highlighted the undeniable power of God's hand in our lives, a force that shields us even in the midst of chaos and danger.

39

The man with the gun, frustrated and bewildered, ran out into a nearby alley, disappearing into the darkness. The weapon had failed to fire, despite his repeated attempts. This wasn't the first time Brother James had experienced divine protection. When he was in his twenties, he had been stabbed during a street altercation. The knife should have pierced vital organs, but it didn't. Instead, it glanced off his ribs, leaving only a superficial wound. **Psalm 34:7 "The angel of the Lord encamps around those who fear him, and he delivers them."** These moments of spiritual warfare reminded me that there are unseen forces at work, both good and evil, but in the midst of it all, God's power is greater.

"I knew then, as I know now, that God was with me, watching over me, protecting me from harm," Brother James said. "He is my shield, my protector, my refuge in times of trouble." This resonated with **Psalm 46:1:** "God is our refuge and strength, a very present help in trouble." As Brother James looked back on these experiences, he saw the hand of God guiding him, keeping him safe, and reminding

Spiritual Awakening 147

him that no matter how dark the world might seem, His light would always shine through.

Reflecting on his early years, Brother James recalled the clash between the teachings of his family and the darker influences of the streets. **"As a child, my mother and family used to force me to go to Sunday school,"** he said. "I remember wondering what all these people were doing, throwing themselves down and seemingly becoming possessed by something unseen. It was unsettling, and I couldn't understand it." The conflicting influences shaped his upbringing, creating a tension between faith and the allure of the streets.

Growing up in Brixton, he was exposed to a lot of African spirituality and heard stories about demonic activity and witchcraft. It was a constant tug-of-war between his family's faith on one side and the street's darker influences on the other. "As I grew older, I began to drift away from what I'd learned in Sunday school," he explained. "The allure of the streets was strong, and I found myself drawn into a world of drugs and crime."

41

Brother James's journey took him far from the teachings of his youth. He started selling drugs, running with gangs, and living a life that was far removed from the guidance he had received as a child. The consequences of his choices were severe—he became entangled in the prison system, his freedom replaced with cell walls and iron bars. It was a stark reminder of the spiritual warfare that ensnares so many, leading them away from the light and into darkness.

Despite the darkness, Brother James found his way back to the Lord. His story was one of redemption and divine protection, illustrating the profound truth found in **Romans 8:28: "And we know that in all things God works for the good of those who love him, who have been called according to his purpose."** His journey from darkness to light is a testament to God's unending grace, a story that will inspire others to seek their own transformation.

As he shared these experiences, I felt a renewed sense of purpose. Brother James's journey had not been easy, but it was filled with moments of divine protection and spiritual awakening. The enemy's tactics were real, but so was the power of God to bring us back from the brink and set us on the path to redemption. As **Ephesians 6:11-13** reminds us, we must put on the full armour of God to stand firm against the schemes of the enemy, knowing that God is always with us, even in our darkest moments. All this before I even hit my twenties. But God has a way of reaching you, even in the darkest places. After my first stint in prison, I met Brother Zechariah, a calm man with a deep understanding of the Word of God. He spoke to me about the higher knowledge contained in the scriptures, opening my eyes to a spiritual world I had ignored for too long. His words planted a seed in my heart, a reminder that there was a better way to live. This idea of planting seeds connects with **Matthew 13:3-8,** where Yahshua tells the parable of the sower, illustrating how the Word of God can take root in the right soil.

When I was released from prison, I was determined to change. I started attending church and diving into the Bible. The teachings of the prophets resonated with me, and I felt the presence of the Holy Spirit guiding my steps. But the path to redemption isn't always straight, and I soon found myself backsliding. The pull of the streets was strong, and I slipped back into old habits. Before I knew it, I was back in prison, feeling like I'd failed myself and God. These experiences remind us that transformation takes time, and it's not always a linear journey. **Proverbs 24:16** states, **"For though the righteous fall seven times, they rise again, but the wicked stumble when calamity strikes."**

Those were dark times, and I struggled with guilt and regret. But even in my lowest moments, I knew that God hadn't abandoned me. I could still hear the echoes of Brother Zechariah's words, reminding me that God's grace is sufficient and that He never gives up on His children. This message aligns with **2 Corinthians 12:9,** where the Lord tells Paul, **"My grace is sufficient for you, for my power is made perfect in weakness."** It's a reminder that even in our weakness, God's strength is made manifest.

It was during my second stint in prison that I truly surrendered my life to God. I realized that spiritual warfare was real, and the only way to overcome it was through faith and obedience. This moment of surrender is crucial in the journey of faith, and it's reflected in **James 4:7, which advises, "Submit yourselves, then, to God. Resist the devil, and he will flee from you."** It's not enough to merely acknowledge spiritual warfare; one must actively choose to resist the enemy and submit to God's authority.

As I continued to share my story with Brother Zechariah, I felt a sense of liberation. The prison walls couldn't contain the freedom that came from knowing Yahshua Christ. **John 8:36 says, "So if the Son sets you free, you will be free indeed."** This was my turning point, my spiritual awakening, and I knew that from then on, my life would be dedicated to serving God and helping others find the same freedom.

The journey from darkness to light is one that requires patience, guidance, and divine intervention. It's a process of growth and learning, where each step forward can be met with setbacks. But with God on our side, even the darkest paths can be illuminated. This chapter illustrates the reality of spiritual warfare and the power of God's grace to transform even the most broken lives. Through prayer, scripture, and obedience, I found my way back to the Lord, and now I seek to share this message of hope and redemption with others who might be walking a similar path.

This time, I was determined to stay on the right path. I started to pray regularly and read the Bible with a new sense of urgency. I made a commitment to turn my life around, not just for myself, but for everyone I had hurt along the way. As I began to walk in the light of God's truth, I felt a sense of peace that I had never known before. The spiritual battles continued, but I knew that with God on my side, I could overcome anything. This transformation aligns with **2 Corinthians 5:17: "Therefore, if anyone is in Christ, the new creation has come: The old has gone, the new is here!"**

Returning to the outside world, I had a renewed sense of purpose. I wanted to share my story, to help others who were struggling with their own battles. I became involved in outreach programs, mentoring young people who were at risk of falling into the same traps I had. I used my experiences to show them that no matter how far you've fallen, there's always a way back. This commitment to outreach reflects **Matthew 5:16,** where Yahshua encourages us to let our light shine before others so they can see our good works and glorify our Father in heaven.

Every day I woke up with gratitude, knowing that God had given me a second chance. Spiritual warfare is ongoing, but I've learned that with faith, community, and a commitment to live according to God's Word, you can find victory even in the toughest battles. My journey is far from over, but I know that with God as my guide, the future is filled with hope. **Romans 8:28** offers reassurance: **"And we know that in all things God works for the good of those who love him, who have been called according to his purpose."**

 The message was simple: No matter how dark it gets, there is always hope in Christ. I emphasized that spiritual warfare is real, but with the right tools—prayer, scripture, and a strong support system—we can resist the enemy's attacks. **Ephesians 6:11-13** reminds us to put on the full armour of God, indicating that the battle against evil requires spiritual preparation.

We can make a difference in the lives of those who were struggling with their own spiritual battles. The call to serve became more than a personal journey; it was a mission to help others find their way back to God.

It's a testament to the enduring grace of God, a reminder that no matter how far we've fallen, there's always a way back. As I continue on this path, I know that the spiritual warfare we face is ongoing, but so is the victory we have in Christ. The road ahead may be challenging, but with faith and determination, we can overcome anything.

Now, every day I wake up with gratitude, knowing that God has given me a second chance. Spiritual warfare is ongoing, but I've learned that with faith, community, and a commitment to live according to God's Word, you can find victory even in the toughest battles. My journey is far from over, but I know that with God as my guide, the future is filled with hope. Being a mentor has given me a new sense of direction. When I speak to young people, I try to be as real as possible about the consequences of the streets. I talk about my time in prison, the friends I lost, and the deep sense of regret that came with it. But I also talk about redemption and how faith can transform even the most broken lives.

The pull of my old life is strong at times, but I keep reminding myself of the miracles I've experienced and the times when God's hand clearly protected me. **Romans 12:2** encourages us not to conform to the pattern of this world, but to be transformed by the renewing of our minds. This transformation isn't easy, but with God's help, it's possible.

"Absolutely. I'm living proof." I explained that spiritual warfare is a constant struggle, but with God's help, we can find the strength to overcome our past and create a new future. **1 John 1:9** assures us that if we confess our sins, God is faithful and just to forgive us and purify us from all unrighteousness.

This armor—truth, righteousness, faith, and the Word of God—is what equips us for the spiritual warfare that we face every day.

It wasn't just about my own transformation; it was about helping others find their way back to God. The path ahead was challenging, but with God's guidance, I knew we could navigate it together, inspiring others to embrace the light and find hope in Christ. This was the message I wanted to share: no matter how dark the past, the future holds the promise of redemption.

I know that sharing my story can make a difference, even if it's just for one person. I often think about the times when I was at my lowest, when I felt like there was no way out. I want to be that same source of hope for others. This resonates with **2 Corinthians 1:3-4,** which says, "Praise be to the God and Father of our Lord Yahshua Christ, the Father of compassion and the God of all comfort, who comforts us in all our troubles, so that we can comfort those in any trouble with the comfort we ourselves receive from God."

Today, I'm more committed than ever to my faith and to helping those who are lost find their way. I know that the journey won't always be easy, and there will be times when I'll stumble. But I also know that I have a community of believers who support me, and, more importantly, I have God on my side. He has already brought me through so much, and I trust that He will continue to guide me as I move forward. **Psalm 23:4** reminds us, **"Even though I walk through the valley of the shadow of death, I will fear no evil, for you are with me; your rod and your staff, they comfort me."** This trust in God's guidance is a cornerstone of my journey.

As I continue to grow in my faith, I look forward to the opportunities to make a positive impact on others. Whether it's through mentorship, speaking engagements, or simply being a good friend, I want to be a light in a world that often feels dark. **Matthew 5:14-16** emphasizes the importance of being a light, encouraging believers to "let your light shine before others, so that they may see your good works and give glory to your Father who is in heaven." I believe that every person has a purpose, and I'm determined to fulfil mine. Because in the end, it's not just about surviving the battles—it's about emerging from them stronger, wiser, and ready to share the light of God's love with the world.

"Wow," I exclaimed as Brother James continued to expand on his experiences. "So tell me, Brother James," I said with genuine interest, "was this the first experience you had with the Holy Spirit?" His journey had been filled with spiritual battles, but his faith remained strong.

"No," he replied, "I've always felt a sense of divine protection through it all. But things got really dark before the light of Christ shined through." He paused for a moment, reflecting on the tumultuous journey that led him to this point. His response reminded me of **Psalm 27:1:** "The Lord is my light and my salvation; whom shall I fear? The Lord is the stronghold of my life; of whom shall I be afraid?" It was clear that his faith had guided him through many trials, and he was now ready to share his testimony to inspire others.

Spiritual Awakening 147

"My sister had a dream," Brother James continued. "She shared it with me, saying it was meant for me. In the dream, I was told that I couldn't serve two masters. I was getting caught up in the streets, pulled in by the allure of fast money and dangerous friends. It was a path I knew I shouldn't be on, but it was hard to resist. The streets can be enticing, but they rarely end well." His sister's dream was a divine warning, echoing **Matthew 6:24,** which states, "No one can serve two masters. Either you will hate the one and love the other, or you will be devoted to the one and despise the other."

He spoke about the chaos of the early days of the COVID-19 pandemic. The lockdowns, the fear, the uncertainty—it was a time when everyone was struggling to find their footing.

"During the 23-hour lockdowns, I had a lot of time to think. I was a chef by trade, but the kitchen was just as chaotic as the streets. It was a battle every day to stay focused and not get pulled back into old habits."

Brother James mentioned how he began to find strength in his faith, even as the world around him seemed to be falling apart. "I was going through a transformation," he said. "I was starting to see the patterns in my life, the times when I'd slipped back into old ways. I knew I had to change, but it wasn't easy. There were relationships that were pulling me in different directions, people who wanted me to stay in the lifestyle I was trying to leave behind." The Apostle Paul writes in **Romans 12:2** about the importance of transformation and renewal of the mind, a theme that resonated with Brother James's journey.

He spoke about how the dream from his sister had been a wake-up call. "It was like God was telling me, 'You can't serve two masters. You can't walk both paths.' It was time to make a choice, and I chose the path of light." This choice to follow the light aligns with **John 8:12,** where Yahshua declares, **"I am the light of the world. Whoever follows me will never walk in darkness, but will have the light of life."**

Brother James began to read the Bible more, finding comfort in its words and drawing closer to the teachings of Christ. "The deeper I went into the Word, the more I felt a spiritual awakening happening within me. I started to see things more clearly, to understand that there are deeper principles at work in this world, and that spiritual warfare is very real." His spiritual awakening echoes **Ephesians 5:14,** which says, "Wake up, sleeper, rise from the dead, and Christ will shine on you."

As he spoke, I could see the passion in his eyes. This wasn't just a story—it was a testimony of faith, redemption, and the power of transformation. "I started to get guidance from the church, from other believers who had walked similar paths," he said. "It helped me stay grounded, to remember that I'm not alone in this journey. There are others who have fought the same battles and come out on the other side." The importance of community and fellowship in spiritual growth is highlighted in **Hebrews 10:24-25**, which encourages believers to "spur one another on toward love and good deeds" and not to neglect meeting together.

Brother James's story is a powerful reminder of the enduring grace of God and the transformative power of faith. His journey from the streets to a life of redemption serves as an inspiration to others who are struggling with their own spiritual battles. By sharing his testimony, he hopes to show others that no matter how far they've wandered, there's always a way back to the light.

Brother James knew that his story wasn't over, that the battles would continue. But he also knew that he was equipped to face them, with the strength that came from his faith and the support of a community that understood his journey. "I don't claim to have all the answers," he said, "but I know that I'm on the right path. And I want to help others find their way too."

It was clear that Brother James had a unique perspective, one shaped by struggle and redemption. His words resonated with me, reminding me that even in the darkest of times, there's always a glimmer of hope, a reason to keep fighting, and a light that can guide us through the storm.

"Then, it was sickness in the spiritual realm," Brother James continued, his voice filled with a mixture of conviction and sorrow. "I felt pain in my body, and I realized it was being revealed to me, not just as a physical ailment but as a sign of spiritual warfare. The pain I was feeling was a manifestation of many things—divisive spirits, negative influences, things holding me back."

He paused, a hint of sadness in his eyes. "I was alone at the time, struggling with bad patterns. Things that made me question everything—why we're pricked at birth, why some people seem cursed or hexed. It was like I was trapped in a cycle, a cycle of darkness that I couldn't break free from."

"At that point," he continued, "a man of God told me I was in a cycle of curses and hexes. He said that when you're alone, that's when the enemy strikes the hardest. When you're isolated, your thoughts can become a battlefield, and it's easy to lose sight of what's real and what's an attack from the enemy. It's like what happened to the Messiah in the wilderness—tempted, tested, pushed to the brink."

Brother James shared how this spiritual battle took a toll on him, but it also taught him valuable lessons. "I've been taught to walk in the Spirit, to seek guidance from the commandments, and to keep my faith strong. It's not easy, especially when you're facing spiritual attacks. There were times when I felt like everything was against me, like people I knew and loved were trying to destroy me and my family. It's real—spiritual warfare is real." He spoke about the importance of discernment, learning to distinguish between his own thoughts and the deceptive thoughts planted by the enemy. "Sometimes you have to know when you're under attack," he said. "The enemy can make you doubt everything—your faith, your worth, your purpose. But if you stay grounded in the Word, you can overcome those lies. You can find the strength to keep going." "People often come to God asking for things," Brother James continued. "But in spiritual warfare, it's not just about asking; it's about trusting. Trusting that the Most High God is the one who protects us, that the angels He sends are real and that they do shield us from harm. But it's also about knowing that the enemy is relentless, and you must be vigilant. You can't let your guard down."

Spiritual Awakening 147

58

As he spoke, I could sense the gravity of his words. This wasn't just a story—it was a warning, a call to be aware of the unseen battles that rage around us. "The enemy will try to throw you off balance," he said. "He'll use anything to break you—fear, doubt, pain, even the people closest to you. But you must remain unshakable. You must remember that God is greater than any curse, any hex, any darkness." His message was clear: spiritual warfare is an ongoing struggle, but with faith, discernment, and the support of a spiritual community, victory is possible. "Ask, and you shall receive," he said. "But you must also fight. You must stand firm, knowing that the Most High God is with you, guiding you through the storm. Because in the end, it's not about how many battles you face—it's about who you have by your side when you face them."

I learned through the Spirit that spiritual warfare requires boldness and discernment. It's not enough to recognize the enemy; you have to know how to counterattack. The enemy's schemes are subtle, and the wickedness they practice often hides in plain sight. I started to realize that it's not just about praying for protection; it's about reclaiming the territory that has been lost and sending back the evil they try to send our way.

We, the chosen ones, are called to speak to God and hear His voice. The power of the Holy Spirit enables us to discern the enemy's tactics and overcome them with God's Word. I don't doubt that wicked people practice witchcraft, even in their own homes. Just take a look at internet —searches about how to perform spells and incantations its everywhere. You'd be surprised how easy it is to find information about the dark arts.

I was shocked to discover that children are being drawn into this world. In dark rooms, away from the light of day, they're taught rituals and ceremonies that have nothing to do with God's plan for their lives. It's not just adults—they're recruiting the next generation to carry on their practices. I knew I had to stand firm and walk in the Spirit to combat this.

Spiritual Awakening 147

60

Yet, in the midst of all this darkness, there's hope. We are children of God, and His Word is unstoppable. The spiritual eye—sometimes called the third eye—enables us to see beyond the physical and recognize spiritual realities. To counter the enemy, you have to be walking in the Spirit, relying on God's guidance and His Word as your shield.

I started to share this revelation with others, declaring the glory of God wherever I went. I told people that the enemy might use fear and deception, but God's truth is a beacon that can't be dimmed. The more I spoke about it, the more I realized that I wasn't alone in this fight. There were others who had seen the same things, experienced the same attacks, and found victory through their faith.

The battle isn't easy, and the enemy doesn't give up without a fight. I had moments when I felt like I was walking through a minefield, unsure of what would come next. But I knew that as long as I stayed close to God, I would be protected. I started to pray more, to read the Bible with new intensity, and to surround myself with others who shared my faith.

Spiritual Awakening 147

I also learned that we must be vigilant. The enemy doesn't just attack us directly; he uses deception to infiltrate our lives in subtle ways.

I began to notice patterns—how certain thoughts and behaviours could be influenced by unseen forces. But by walking in the Spirit, I could discern these influences and resist them.

WE SERVE A POWERFUL GOD

Spiritual Awakening 147

Chapter 4: Declaring the Glory of God

This chapter of my life taught me that spiritual warfare is not just about defence; it's about offence. It's about declaring the glory of God in the face of adversity and standing firm in the knowledge that He is greater than any darkness. I knew that I had a responsibility to share this message with others, to open their eyes to the realities of spiritual warfare and to equip them with the tools to overcome.

As I moved forward, I realized that I was not just fighting for myself—I was fighting for my family, my friends, and everyone who needed to hear the truth. The battle continues, but I'm ready for it. Because I know that as long as I keep my eyes on God and walk in the Spirit, there's nothing the enemy can do to stop me from declaring the glory of God. It was one of those nights when sleep eluded me. I was lying in my bedroom, my mind racing with thoughts that felt like they weren't even mine. They were dark, twisted, and violent—bare evil thoughts. It was the kind of madness that makes you wonder if you're losing your grip on reality. I tried to rebuke the thoughts, to push them out of my mind, but they just kept coming, one after the other.

It was about five in the morning when my phone rang out of nowhere. The ringtone pierced through the silence, jarring me out of my spiralling thoughts. It was strange, though —I didn't recognize the number, and no one usually calls me at that hour. As the phone kept ringing, I felt a presence in the room, a divine call that lifted me, filling me with a sense of power. It was as if God had entered the room, surrounding me with His light.

I sat up, heart racing, and said, "Lord, I am the Lord your God. What's happening? Why am I being attacked like this?" The intensity of the moment was overwhelming, but the sense of divine presence was even stronger. It felt like I was standing at a crossroads, and the path I chose could change everything.

Then, I heard the Lord's voice in my spirit. He told me that the attacks were connected to the weed I had been smoking. It hit me like a ton

Spiritual Awakening 147

of bricks—the realization that something seemingly harmless could be opening a doorway to dark forces. I had always thought of weed as a way to relax, to escape from the stresses of life, but I never considered that it might be causing more harm than good.

I started to understand that the spiritual realm is more complex than I had imagined. The weed I was smoking wasn't just affecting my body; it was affecting my spirit. It was clouding my mind, making it easier for the enemy to plant those evil thoughts. I had heard stories about how drugs could open people up to spiritual influences, but I never thought it could happen to me.

The Lord made it clear that I needed to stop, that I couldn't allow anything to compromise my spiritual journey. The attacks I was experiencing in my bedroom were real, and they were connected to the choices I was making. It was a wake-up call, a moment of clarity that I couldn't ignore.

I started to pray more, seeking guidance and strength to resist the temptation of the weed. I knew it wouldn't be easy—habits like that don't break overnight. But I was determined to cut it out of my life, to close the door that had been opened to the enemy.

As I began to change my habits, the attacks in my bedroom became less frequent. The darkness that had once filled my mind began to lift, replaced by a sense of peace and clarity. I knew I was on the right path, but I also knew that the enemy would try to find other ways to attack.

In the weeks that followed, I kept my focus on God, reading the Bible and praying for protection. I could feel the spiritual warfare continuing, but I was better equipped to handle it. I was no longer relying on substances to cope with life—I was relying on God's strength.

The battle with evil thoughts wasn't over, but I was no longer fighting it alone. I had the presence of the Lord with me, guiding me through the storm. And with each passing day, I grew stronger, more resilient, and more determined to walk in the light. The problem with intoxication it can weaken you spiritually opening you to attacks the bible says be sober

Spiritual Awakening 147

minded 1st Peter 5 8-9 these think you're in control when, in reality, you're opening yourself up to forces that seek to destroy you. And with each passing day, I grew stronger, more resilient, and more determined to walk in the light. The problem with intoxication is that it can weaken you spiritually, opening you to attacks. The Bible warns us to be sober-minded: "Be sober, be vigilant; because your adversary the devil walks about like a roaring lion, seeking whom he may devour. Resist him, steadfast in the faith, knowing that the same sufferings are experienced by your brotherhood in the world" (1 Peter 5:8-9).

When we think we are in control, intoxication deceives us, making us vulnerable to forces that seek to destroy us. As Proverbs 20:1 says, "Wine is a mocker, strong drink is raging: and whosoever is deceived thereby is not wise." To guard our hearts and minds, we must remain vigilant and sober, aligning ourselves with the will of God and standing firm in His protection. Ephesians 5:18 further advises, "And do not be drunk with wine, in which is dissipation; but be filled with the Spirit." By doing so, we can walk in the light, fortified against spiritual attacks, and grow in strength and determination. I learned that the hard way, but I also learned that with God on your side, there's nothing you can't overcome.

Just look online—it's not hard to find instructions for witchcraft, and even kids are learning it. You'd be surprised how many people are dabbling in this stuff. I wouldn't put it past them to tamper with anything, even weed." He continued, "Think about it—sometimes even products that are regulated on TV get recalled because there's something wrong with them. If that can happen to products under strict regulations, imagine what people could be doing with substances like weed, where there's less oversight. This thing goes really deep, brother." I hummed in agreement, encouraging him to continue. "Preach, Brother James," I said, watching as his tone began to shift slightly. There was a hint of his ancestral Jamaican roots in his voice as he testified. "I don't know why I come this far," he said, "but the God of Heaven is a holy God, and we have to be a holy people. A wise man once told me I have to be a holy vessel for Him to use. You understand?"

There was a moment of silence, but I felt the Holy Spirit telling me to remain quiet, so I did. I took a deep breath, sensing that Brother James was about to share something important. He continued, "The path of sin only leads to destruction. You can see it in the prisons, in the people who are lost and broken. When I wake up now in the Spirit, I can see the spirits on people. Some of them are so far from God, and they're getting destroyed because they're not walking in the Spirit."

He was right—there was a visible change in people who had turned away from God, a darkness that seemed to follow them. Brother James mentioned that he had learned an important lesson from his sister: "You can't serve two masters," he said. "You can't be lukewarm, because the Bible says that if you're lukewarm, He will spit you out."

Brother James continued, his voice full of conviction. "You can't play both sides," he said. "If you try, you'll end up serving the wrong master, and that's a road you don't want to go down. It's time for us to be bold in our faith, to walk in the Spirit and declare the glory of God without hesitation. If you don't, you're opening the door for the enemy to take over."

As I listened to him, I realized that this was the spiritual awakening he was talking about—the moment when you understand that you can't live a double life. You have to choose God, and you have to walk in His ways, or you'll find yourself spiralling into a darkness you might not escape from.

Brother James concluded by saying, "The enemy doesn't play games. He'll use anything he can to lead you astray. But if you stay grounded in God's Word, if you keep your faith strong and walk in the Spirit, there's nothing he can do to stop you. Just remember, you can't serve two masters. It's either God or the world—choose wisely."

"Wow, man of God, this is a powerful testimonial," I said to Brother James. "The healing, the spiritual awakening—it's inspiring. Please, share more about your journey."

Brother James nodded, his eyes filled with a mix of determination and gratitude. "Let me tell you, brother," he said, "I didn't come to this understanding overnight. It was a journey—a painful one at times—but it was necessary to bring me to where I am today. My spiritual awakening led me to understand the path I should follow, the true lineage of the Messiah."

He took a deep breath before continuing. "I started to dig deeper into the origins of the faith, to learn about the ancient traditions and the roots of Christianity. That's when I discovered the original name of Christ—Yahshua—and how it had been changed over time. The addition of the 'J'—it's not just a linguistic thing; it's part of a broader shift away from the original teachings."

I could see the passion in his eyes as he spoke. "My spiritual awakening revealed to me who I truly am and who my people are. All glory to God for that revelation—that we are the true Hebrew Israelites. The Lord Himself told me, 'I am the Lord your God,' and I knew it was time to embrace my heritage and my identity."

He mentioned his ancestors, tracing his lineage back to the slave lands of Jamaica. "Our history is tied to the scriptures," he said. "If you look at **Deuteronomy 28**, you'll see the prophecies, the curses, and the promises that were made to the children of Israel. My ancestors fit those descriptions. The suffering, the displacement, the struggle—it's all there in the Bible, and it's a story that's been passed down through generations."

Brother James leaned in, his voice low but firm. "It's important for us to recognize our roots, to understand that we're part of something much larger than ourselves. The prophecies in **Deuteronomy 28** were not just warnings; they were a call to return to the Lord, to walk in His ways, and to reclaim our identity as His chosen people."

I nodded, feeling the weight of his words. The journey of spiritual awakening is often challenging, but it's a path that leads to profound truths and deeper connections with God. "Educate them, Brother James," I encouraged him, knowing that his story could inspire others to seek the truth and embrace their spiritual heritage.

He smiled, a sense of peace in his expression. "I'm not here to preach," he said, "but I know that sharing my story can make a difference. If I can help even one person find their way back to God, to understand their true identity, then it's worth it. We all have a role to play in this spiritual journey, and it's up to us to walk in the light and share the good news with the world."

Brother James' testimonial reminded me that the path to spiritual awakening is unique for each person, but it's a journey worth taking. It requires courage, humility, and a willingness to embrace the truth, even when it's uncomfortable. Ultimately, it's about finding your place in God's plan and living a life that honours Him. Reclaiming the Hebrew Heritage

"The first mention of a Hebrew in the Bible is Abraham," Brother James said as we discussed the roots of the faith. I interjected, "What about Adam? Wasn't he the first man created by God?" Brother James raised an eyebrow, then replied, "Back it up with scripture. Find some verses for me."

Spiritual Awakening 147

I immediately thought of **Isaiah 41:1,** where it talks about gathering from the four corners of the earth. "This verse says that the Lord will gather His people from the ends of the earth," I explained. Brother James nodded, adding, "That's what we see happening now, with people from all over the world awakening to their Hebrew heritage."

We continued our discussion, examining the biblical prophecies about the scattering of the Hebrew people. **"Deuteronomy 28** talks about the curses that would come upon Israel if they disobeyed God," Brother James said. "It mentions that the people would be scattered among all nations. This is a fact—my people are waking up all over the world. They're realizing who they are and where they come from."

"The genetic lineage is mixed now, but that doesn't change the truth about who the Hebrews were. And the scriptures often describe them as dark-skinned."

Look how Yahshua is often depicted in Western art and how it doesn't always align with historical and biblical descriptions. "Many establishments have hidden the images of a black Yahshua, but some are starting to reveal him," Brother James said. "If you ask to see these depictions, they might show you. It's important to understand that the portrayal of Yahshua should not be limited by race or culture."

I nodded, acknowledging the complex history of the depiction of religious figures. "Hebrew isn't just a race; it's a way of life, a people descended from a particular lineage. With the transatlantic slave trade and the Arabian slave trade, many descendants were scattered, but God knows His people, Brother James reminding me that the spiritual journey is about reconnecting with our heritage and seeking redemption. "We have to stay in the Spirit," he said. "Fasting and praying are essential because we face spiritual battles every day. Like in the movie 'War Room,' we need to create our own spiritual force field through prayer and faith."

The power of the tongue, which **James 3:5-6 refers to as a "small part of the body, but it makes great boasts."** "Our words carry power," Brother James explained. "We need to be careful about what we say and how we use our words. The enemy listens and tries to use our words against us."

As we wrapped up this chapter, realize that the journey to reclaiming our Hebrew heritage is both personal and communal. It's about finding the truth in the scriptures and understanding the deeper meanings behind biblical stories. Brother James and I agreed that the path forward involves staying grounded in faith, fasting, and praying, and surrounding ourselves with people who encourage us in our spiritual growth.

The journey of spiritual awakening is never easy, but it's filled with moments of revelation and understanding. It's about recognizing the challenges we face and embracing the call to be holy, as we are part of a lineage that goes back to the beginning of time. As we walk this path, we must stay true to our faith, knowing that the Most High God is guiding us every step of the way.

Chapter 5: Reclaiming the Hebrew Heritage

Brother James had always been a passionate speaker, but this time was different. As he spoke, there was a sudden shift in his tone, a change that signalled the Holy Spirit was moving through him. It was as if a new energy had taken over, lifting the room into a realm of spiritual power. He began to testify about the Lord Most High, Yah, and the message he shared struck a deep chord with everyone listening.

"We must do good things for each other," he said, his voice filled with conviction. "The God of Heaven is a holy God, and we must be a holy people. We must be holy vessels for Him to use." He paused, as if to let the words sink in, then continued with even greater intensity. "I don't know why I've come this far, but I'm here to tell you that the path of sin only leads to destruction."

Brother James spoke about his time in prison, the despair and chaos that surrounded him, and how he saw the destruction it caused in the lives of others. "When I wake up now, I can see the destruction in people's lives, and it's clear that they are not being led by the Lord. If you're not in the Holy Spirit, something else will be leading you. I've learned that you can't serve two masters—either you're with God, or you're not. The lukewarm He will spit out."

This revelation had been shared with him by his sister, and it led to a spiritual awakening that changed his life. He explained how the Lord had shown him the true lineage of the Hebrew people and how he discovered that the original name of Yahshua didn't contain the letter 'J'—it was Yahshua in the Hebrew. "Glory to the Most High Yah," he proclaimed. "The Lord told me that He is the Lord, our God, and that we are His chosen people."

His ancestors came from the slave lands of Jamaica, a history that resonated with the prophecies in **Deuteronomy 28.** The chapter speaks of the scattering of God's people due to disobedience, but it also promises that they will be gathered again from the four corners of the earth. This promise gave Brother James hope, a reason to believe that the Hebrews would return to their rightful place.

The twelve tribes of Israel are named after the twelve sons of Jacob (also known as Israel). Here is the list of the twelve tribes along with their lineage in the order of their birth, according to the Bible:

Reuben
Mother: Leah
Lineage: Jacob → Reuben
Simeon
Mother: Leah
Lineage: Jacob → Simeon

Levi
Mother: Leah
Lineage: Jacob → Levi

Judah
Mother: Leah
Lineage: Jacob → Judah

Dan
Mother: Bilhah (Rachel's maidservant)
Lineage: Jacob → Dan

Naphtali
Mother: Bilhah (Rachel's maidservant)
Lineage: Jacob → Naphtali

Gad
Mother: Zilpah (Leah's maidservant)
Lineage: Jacob → Gad

Asher
Mother: Zilpah (Leah's maidservant)
Lineage: Jacob → Asher

Issachar
Mother: Leah
Lineage: Jacob → Issachar

Zebulun
Mother: Leah
Lineage: Jacob → Zebulun

Joseph
Mother: Rachel
Lineage: Jacob → Joseph
Sons: Ephraim and Manasseh (who were adopted by Jacob and became two of the tribes, replacing Joseph)

Benjamin
Mother: Rachel
Lineage: Jacob → Benjamin

When the land of Israel was divided among the tribes, the tribe of Levi was given no specific territory because their role was to serve as priests and caretakers of the Tabernacle. Instead, the two sons of Joseph, Ephraim and Manasseh, each became a tribe, effectively

Spiritual Awakening 147

replacing the tribe of Joseph and maintaining the number of tribes at twelve.

Thus, the twelve tribes for the purposes of land division are often listed as:

Reuben
Simeon
Judah
Issachar
Zebulun
Dan
Naphtali
Gad
Asher
Ephraim (Joseph)
Manasseh (Joseph)
Benjamin

As the discussion continued, he mentioned the Igbo tribe and other groups in Africa that claim Israelite heritage. He also spoke of the Cushitic and other tribes that have intermingled worldwide, emphasizing that despite the genetic mixing, the truth of the Hebrew lineage remains intact. "The Bible speaks from a Hebrew standpoint and reveals the truth about the scattering of God's people," he said. "It's clear in the scriptures that the people were dark-skinned, with curly, woolly hair."

Spiritual Awakening 147

When I asked Brother James how he felt about the hidden sacred pictures and artefacts that are often concealed from public view, he said, "We know the truth, even if others try to hide it.

People create images that suit their own narrative, but the real truth is in the scriptures and the historical evidence that supports it. Man tries to make God in his own image, but it's not the truth."

Our conversation delved into the significance of these hidden truths and the responsibility of believers to seek out and share the authentic story. Brother James urged everyone to approach these matters with an open heart and a spirit of discernment. "The enemy will try to confuse us and lead us astray," he said. "But we must stay rooted in God's Word and seek the guidance of the Holy Spirit."

Birthright and Blessings

Reuben was Jacob's firstborn, but he lost his birthright due to an indiscretion **(Genesis 35:22; 1 Chronicles 5:1).**

Judah received the leadership role and the blessing of kingship. Jacob's prophetic blessing upon Judah indicated that the scepter (a symbol of royal authority) would not depart from Judah, and it is from this tribe that the line of the Messiah would come **(Genesis 49:8-12).**

Lineage of the Messiah

Abraham: God promised that all nations would be blessed through his descendants **(Genesis 12:3)**

Isaac: The promised son of Abraham (Genesis **17:19)**

Jacob (Israel): The son of Isaac, who fathered the twelve tribes of Israel **(Genesis 28:14).**

Judah: One of the twelve sons of Jacob. The Messianic prophecy indicated that Judah would hold the scepter and the ruler's staff would come from him **(Genesis 49:10).**

Perez: One of the twin sons of Judah and **Tamar (Genesis 38:29).**

Hezron: Son of Perez **(Ruth 4:18-22).**

Ram: Son of Hezron **(Ruth 4:19).**

Amminadab: Son of Ram **(Ruth 4:19-20).**

Nahshon: Son of Amminadab **(Ruth 4:20).**

Salmon: Son of Nahshon **(Ruth 4:20-21).**

Boaz: Son of Salmon, who married Ruth **(Ruth 4:21).**

Obed: Son of Boaz and Ruth **(Ruth 4:21-22).**

Jesse: Son of Obed **(Ruth 4:22).**

David: Son of Jesse, the second king of Israel. God made a covenant with David, promising that his throne would be established forever **(2 Samuel 7:12-16).**

Solomon: Son of David, who succeeded him as king **(1 Chronicles 28:5).**

Lineage of Yahshua
The New Testament traces the lineage of Jesus through the tribe of Judah, fulfilling the Messianic prophecies. Both genealogies in the New Testament **(Matthew 1:1-16 and Luke 3:23-38)** trace Jesus' ancestry through David, affirming His royal lineage.

Matthew: Focuses on the legal lineage through Joseph, showing Jesus' right to the throne of David.

Luke: Often thought to trace the biological lineage through Mary, also showing descent from David.

Therefore, Jesus Christ, the Messiah, is identified as the "Lion of the tribe of Judah" **(Revelation 5:5),** fulfilling the prophecy and the special status given to Judah.

This chapter in Brother James' journey is a testament to the power of spiritual awakening and the importance of walking in the path of holiness. His story reminds us that despite the challenges and the forces that seek to pull us away, the truth will always find its way to those who earnestly seek it.

Brother James had a powerful way of emphasizing the greatness of our people. "We are a mighty, prestigious people," he said, his voice resonating with a sense of pride and purpose. He spoke about the history that led to this moment of awakening, the journey that brought us to a deeper understanding of our identity and heritage. "This truth brings joy, and it's a joy worth sharing," he added.

Brother James spoke of the 12 tribes that were scattered after the second exile. "We may not know exactly where they all went," he said, "but we are dealing with their descendants now, scattered near and far throughout generations. Though there's been a lot of mixing, the Most High God knows who His people are."

Brother James mentioned the advancements in DNA testing, suggesting that with modern technology, we can trace our genetics more accurately. This technology helps uncover the deep roots that connect us to our heritage. He brought up the Atlantic slave trade and the earlier Arabian slave trade, both of which contributed to the dispersal and intermingling of various peoples. Yet despite this, the underlying lineage remains intact.

Brother James explained that this happened because our forefathers worshipped idols, married foreign wives, and served other gods. These actions led to the Israelites losing their spiritual focus and, ultimately, their land.

Brother James emphasized that much of the witchcraft and practices that we see today are rooted in ancient traditions. He warned that the holy feasts and celebrations of the Lord were transformed into secular events, like Halloween, which have little to do with their original sacred meaning. "The world took the holy feasts and twisted them into something entirely different," he said. "They replaced true worship with customs that lead people away from God."

This revealed the complexities of our heritage and the challenges we face in reclaiming the truth. Brother James encouraged us to stay vigilant, to seek out the authentic stories and scriptures that remind us of who we are and who God has called us to be. He also reminded us to be cautious about the cultural influences that attempt to reshape our faith and to stay grounded in the teachings of the Most High God.

Ultimately, this journey is about rediscovering the truth and living in a way that honours our spiritual heritage. It's about acknowledging the mistakes of the past and learning from them, so we don't repeat them. And it's about embracing the identity that God has given us, with all its power and prestige, to walk the path of righteousness and share the light with the world.

Brother James was on fire, his voice ringing with urgency and conviction. "Follow Christ, brothers and sisters," he declared, his words echoing through the room. "The only way to eternal life is in Christ. He is the path, the truth, and the life."

As he spoke, he recalled the words of Yahshua: **"If they chopped down the tree, what do you think they'll do with the branches?"** It was a stark reminder that if Christ, the source of life and truth, suffered for our sins, then we, as His followers, must be prepared for the same trials and persecution. "We are branches," Brother James said, "and our strength comes from our connection to the tree. Without Christ, we wither and die. We must stay rooted in Him, drawing our nourishment from His Word and His Spirit."

Brother James then turned his attention to the story of Cain and Abel, a tragic account of the first recorded murder in the Bible. He explained how Cain, by slaying his brother, opened a spiritual portal that allowed evil to seep into the world. "When you choose hate

Spiritual Awakening 147

over love, violence over peace, you invite darkness into your heart," he said. "Cain's act of violence against Abel wasn't just a crime against his brother—it was a rejection of God's way."

He urged us to follow the path of Yahshua, to walk in the footsteps of Yahshua, who taught us to love our Neighbors and forgive our enemies. "This journey isn't just about words," he said. "It's about living in the Spirit, letting it guide our thoughts and actions. It's about more than just going to church—it's about having a living relationship with God."

The message was clear: spiritual growth requires continuous effort. "We have to work on it," Brother James said. "Pray, fast, read your Bible, and keep your spirit man alive." He encouraged us to spend time in prayer and meditation, seeking God's guidance in all aspects of life. Fasting, he explained, was a way to disconnect from the physical and focus on the spiritual. "When you fast, you deny the flesh to feed the spirit. It's a discipline that draws you closer to God."

Reading the Bible was another essential practice. "The Word of God is living and active," he said. "It speaks to us, guides us, and equips us for the battles we face. We need to keep the scriptures in our hearts and minds, using them as a sword against the enemy's lies."

Brother James's words were a call to action, a reminder that following Christ is a daily commitment. He spoke about the importance of community and fellowship, of surrounding ourselves with like-minded believers who can support and encourage us. "We can't do this alone," he said. "We need each other, just as the branches need the tree. Together, we are stronger."

As the evening drew to a close, I felt a renewed sense of purpose and determination. The road ahead wouldn't be easy, but with Christ as our guide, we could face any challenge. Brother James's message reminded me that the path of righteousness is a journey, one that requires constant vigilance and commitment.

In the end, it's not just about avoiding sin—it's about embracing the light, choosing love over hate, and living in a way that reflects the teachings of Christ. It's about being a holy vessel, as Brother James said, for God to use.

Spiritual Awakening 147

Brother James spoke about the presence of different entities within people, suggesting that these spiritual battles are not always visible but can be sensed by those with spiritual discernment. He emphasized that the Word of God is our weapon against these unseen forces, a guiding light that helps us navigate the complexities of spiritual warfare.

The Hebrew language has deep roots in spiritual meaning and history. There is a saying among the Hebrews that speaks to the essence of their souls. Brother James delved into the origin of certain names, like James translated to Jacob and finally **Yaakov (Jacob),** which means "he who supplants" or "held by the heel." This name is derived from the biblical story of Jacob and Esau, twin brothers with a complicated relationship. Jacob was born holding onto Esau's heel, symbolizing his role as a supplanter or someone who takes another's place.

Brother James explained that names carry significance, often reflecting one's destiny or purpose. The name "James" itself, derived from Latin, carries the meaning "may God protect," highlighting the spiritual connection between names and their meanings. This deeper understanding of names ties into the broader narrative of spiritual warfare—how individuals are shaped by their identities, both spiritual and cultural.

As we continued our discussion, Brother James shared insights into how the manipulation of names and language can impact spiritual understanding. He mentioned that the letter "J" was introduced into the English language, changing the original Hebrew names, which can alter the perception of biblical narratives. "The introduction of new elements into our language can create confusion," he said. "It's like a subtle shift that can lead us away from the original truth."

The conversation took a deeper turn as we explored the implications of these changes. Brother James pointed out that certain terms and concepts might be designed to divert people from understanding their true heritage and connection to God. "The enemy works in subtle ways," he said. "He can use language to distort our perception, to create doubt, and to lead us away from the path of righteousness."

We discussed the importance of staying rooted in the Word of God and seeking guidance from the Holy Spirit. "It's not just about what we say—it's about how we live," Brother James emphasized. "We need to be vigilant, to discern the enemy's tactics, and to hold fast to the truth." He encouraged us to examine the scriptures, to seek out the original meanings, and to be wary of modern interpretations that might not align with the original intent.

The conversation touched on the idea of being sons and daughters of God, emphasizing that our spiritual heritage is what defines us. Brother James urged us to embrace this identity, to walk in the Spirit, and to use our names as a reminder of our purpose. "Your name is a reflection of who you are," he said. "It's a declaration of your identity in Christ."

As we concluded our discussion, it became clear that the battle against spiritual forces requires more than just knowledge—it requires faith, commitment, and a deep connection to God. Brother James's words resonated with me, reminding me that spiritual warfare is a journey, one that demands constant vigilance and a willingness to stand firm in the face of adversity. The enemy may try to undermine our faith, but with the Word of God as our guide, we can overcome any challenge.

Chapter 6: Walking in the Spirit

It's a light that the enemy is trying to break in," Brother James said, his voice crackling over the phone. "You have to fight to keep the prayer life strong, to keep the fullness of the Spirit." His words resonated with a sense of urgency, the kind that comes from knowing you're in a battle where the stakes are high.

He asked me if I'd seen the film "War Room," a story about the power of prayer and spiritual warfare. "That's the level you need to get on in this battle," he said. "It's not just a physical struggle—it's spiritual. When you do God's work, you need to get the knowledge and fight the good fight. Don't let the enemy get back in."

Brother James continued, warning me about the subtle ways the enemy tries to infiltrate. "Some people who speak in tongues, it's not always of the Lord," he cautioned. "We need to learn how powerful our tongues are. We can speak life or death with our words, so be careful what you say. Call on protection, and listen to the Spirit for guidance. Spiritual awakening is crucial for strengthening your relationship with the Lord."

Spiritual Awakening 147

I asked him when he first felt the presence of the Lord. He paused for a moment, as if recalling a vivid memory, then said, "I've had so much intervention in my life. When I was hurt, I cried out to God, and He lifted me out of the pain. There was one night I fell asleep in agony, tossing and turning, fighting the spiritual attacks. I remember it like yesterday."

He spoke about a night when he was struggling with intense pain, both physical and spiritual. It felt like a battle was raging within him, and he was losing. "I was tossing and turning," he said, "feeling the weight of the enemy pressing down on me. But then, in the early hours of the morning, I heard a phone ringing. It was a strange sound—ding, ding, ding—and I knew it wasn't just a normal call."

He continued, "I answered the phone in a lucid state, and suddenly, I felt my body being lifted up. It was as if I was floating, and then I heard the voice of the Lord, clear as day: 'I am the Lord your God.' That moment changed everything. It was like the darkness had no more power over me."

Brother James also shared other times when the Lord revealed crucial information to him.

Spiritual Awakening 147

"There have been moments when He showed me who was working against me in the spirit," he said. "These attacks are meant to hinder us, to slow us down, but they can't stop the will of the Lord. We need to remember that He is with us, even when it feels like we're alone."

The conversation turned reflective as Brother James spoke about how these divine interventions had transformed his life. "It's not just about the big moments," he said. "It's about the everyday commitment to serve Him and remember that His Son came and died for us. That sacrifice is what gives us the strength to keep fighting."

As I listened to Brother James, I realized that spiritual warfare is an ongoing battle, one that requires constant vigilance and a deep connection with God. It's not enough to know the scriptures—you have to live them, embodying the principles of faith and righteousness. The enemy is always looking for a way in, but with the Lord on your side, you have the power to resist.

This chapter in Brother James's journey is a testament to the power of prayer, faith, and divine intervention. It reminds us that the spiritual battle is real, but so is the protection and guidance that come from the Lord. We must stay strong, call on His name, and trust that no matter how intense the battle becomes, the light of God will always prevail.

The desire to share my testimony with the whole world was overwhelming. I wanted people to understand the reality of spiritual warfare and the techniques to combat it. Brother James's words had inspired me, but I knew I had to do more than just listen—I had to act.

"I must tell you how I overcame and how I'm dealing with the spiritual attacks now," He said, taking a deep breath. The spiritual journey was intense, filled with challenges and trials, but it had also brought me closer to God. I was ready to share what I had learned.

First, I knuckled down in faith. This wasn't just about attending church on Sundays—it was about immersing myself in the Word of God. The more I read the Bible, the clearer it became that spiritual warfare was an everyday battle. It wasn't just something from ancient times; it was happening right now, in the midst of our modern lives. I began to see the "matrix," the unseen forces at play in this world, and I realized that the beast was active and constantly seeking to lead us astray.

"Open your eyes to the matrix," "Once you're awake, you realize how much is happening beneath the surface." The enemy was subtle, using distractions, temptations, and doubt to try and derail my faith. But I knew that the only way to overcome was to stay rooted in God, to pray without ceasing, and to seek His guidance in everything I did.

Brother James nodded, acknowledging that spiritual attacks are a constant threat. "Are you still getting attacked now?" I asked. His response was straightforward: "It's never really gonna fully stop. But you're in training, and you'll grow in strength as you keep on the path." It was a reminder that the journey doesn't end, but it does get easier as you grow in faith and spiritual maturity.

The key to overcoming spiritual attacks, I learned, was to stay vigilant and committed to spiritual growth. Prayer, fasting, and studying the Bible were my main weapons. I also made it a point to surround myself with people who shared my faith, creating a supportive community that could help me stay strong when the attacks came. "The enemy will try to take you off the path," Brother James said. "But it's our mission, as those who are spiritually awake, to awaken others out of darkness."

Spiritual warfare isn't something to be taken lightly. It's a battle for your soul, and the stakes are high. But I found strength in knowing that God was with me, that His angels were watching over me, and that He had equipped me with the tools to fight back. I began to recognize the signs of spiritual attacks—sudden doubts, unexpected obstacles, and moments of intense temptation—and I learned to combat them with prayer and the Word of God.

One of the most important techniques I used was to declare the promises of God out loud. By speaking His Word, I could push back against the darkness and reaffirm my faith. I also practice gratitude, thanking God for His protection and guidance, even in the midst of trials. This mindset shift helped me stay positive and focused on the bigger picture.

"Spiritual warfare is real," but so is the victory we have in Christ." I knew that my testimony could help others, that by sharing my experiences, I could encourage those who were struggling. The path ahead wasn't easy, but I was determined to stay on it, to keep growing in faith, and to help others do the same.

The journey of spiritual awakening is a continuous process. It's about learning, growing, and becoming stronger in the face of adversity. It's about recognizing that the enemy is always at work, but so is God, and His power is far greater than any darkness. By staying rooted in faith and using the techniques I learned, I knew I could overcome any spiritual attack that came my way.

Chapter 7: Power of Words and the Tongue

The desire to share my testimony with the whole world was overwhelming. I wanted people to understand the reality of spiritual warfare and the techniques to combat it.

"I must tell you how I overcame and how I'm dealing with the spiritual attacks now," I said, taking a deep breath. The spiritual journey was intense, filled with challenges and trials, but it had also brought me closer to God. I was ready to share what I had learned.

First, I knuckled down in faith. This wasn't just about attending church on Sundays—it was about immersing myself in the Word of God. The more I read the Bible, the clearer it became that spiritual warfare was an everyday battle. It wasn't just something from ancient times; it was happening right now, in the midst of our modern lives. I began to see the "matrix," the unseen forces at play in this world, and I realized that the beast was active and constantly seeking to lead us astray.

"Yahshua HaMashiach is our Saviour, and there's no way we're gonna go back to sleep," Brother James declared with unwavering conviction. "The Bible is the truth, the foundation of everything we believe in. We're all under divine guidance, within God's power, and all glory be to the Most High."

His words filled the room with a sense of certainty and strength. The light of faith had broken through, and Brother James was determined to keep that light burning. "From the dust we came, and to the dust we will return," he said, "but while we're here, we must serve the Lord with all our heart, mind, and soul."

He reminded us that God is in control, even when it seems like the wicked are prospering. "Every great king—from Pharaoh to Nebuchadnezzar—God brought them down if they were wicked or too proud. The Word of God is the ultimate authority. Follow the path, and you'll never go wrong."

Brother James spoke about the importance of prayer and learning to pray on a new level. He encouraged us to develop a strong prayer life, one that could withstand the attacks of the enemy. "When you pray," he said, "you're not just speaking words—you're engaging in spiritual warfare. You have to pray with purpose, with passion, and with faith that God will hear and answer."

As he spoke, the energy in the room intensified. The Spirit was clearly at work, turning what was supposed to be a brief discussion into a full-fledged sermon.

"Wow, Brother James, thank you," I said, offering him a moment to catch his breath. It was miraculous how a 30-minute schedule had turned into something so much more profound.

Spiritual Awakening 147

"This is more like a movie," I added, marveling at the depth of the conversation. "I'm sure a director would be interested in taking this on."

Brother James laughed, a genuine, joyful sound that echoed through the space. "It's the power of the Holy Spirit," he said. "When God moves, things happen. And it's all for His glory."

He encouraged us to keep walking in the Spirit, to stay on the path that leads to righteousness, and to remain steadfast in our faith. "We can't let the world distract us," he said. "There's too much at stake. Keep your focus on Yahshua HaMashiach, and you'll find the strength to overcome anything."

Brother James's words had inspired me, but I knew I had to do more than just listen—I had to act. With renewed determination, I began to integrate Brother James's teachings into my daily life. The first step was to enhance my prayer life. Instead of treating prayer as a mere ritual, I started to see it as a powerful tool for spiritual warfare. Every morning, I dedicated time to pray fervently, pouring out my heart and seeking divine guidance. I prayed for protection, for wisdom, and for the strength to resist the temptations and deceptions of the enemy. In the stillness of the night, Brother James led us in prayer. "Father, we come before You, humbling ourselves and seeking Your face. We ask for Your Holy Spirit to fill this place, to fill us. We need Your power, Lord, to overcome the battles we face."

As we prayed, a sense of unity and purpose enveloped us. We were not just individuals; we were a spiritual family, bound together by our faith and our commitment to the Kingdom of God. The next day was spent in fasting and prayer, interspersed with sessions of Bible study and worship. Each session was a step deeper into the presence of God, a step closer to understanding His will for our lives.

Brother James reminded us of our mission. "Go forth in the power of the Spirit," he urged. "Remember, you are not alone. We stand together, and more importantly, God is with us." The spiritual attacks didn't stop, but I was no longer afraid. I knew I was equipped, not just to survive, but to thrive. I was part of a mighty army, standing on the hill of faith, ready to face whatever came my way. And with Yahshua HaMashiach as our leader, we could not fail.

Spiritual Awakening 147

Chapter 8: The Armor of God

The weeks following the retreat were a testament to the power of prayer and unity. Each day, I felt more fortified, more prepared for the spiritual battles that lay ahead. The lessons I had learned were not just theoretical; they were practical, and they were life-changing. The enemy's attacks were relentless, but now I had the tools and the faith to stand firm.

One evening, as the sun dipped below the horizon, casting a golden glow over the city, I sat down with my journal to reflect on my journey. The words of Brother James echoed in my mind: "We are a mighty army, clad in the armor of light." I realized that it was time to delve deeper into what that armor truly meant.

Ephesians 6:10-18 had always been a familiar passage, but now it took on a new significance. The Armor of God was not just a metaphor; it was a spiritual reality, a divine protection that we had to consciously put on every day.

"Finally, be strong in the Lord and in his mighty power. Put on the full armor of God, so that you can take your stand against the devil's schemes." As I read these verses, I felt a renewed sense of purpose. The battle was real, but so was the protection God provided.

The first piece of armor, the belt of truth, was foundational. In a world filled with deception, the truth of God's Word was our anchor. I committed myself to daily study, ensuring that my mind was girded with divine truth. Lies and half-truths could not stand against the clarity and power of Scripture.

Next, the breastplate of righteousness. This was about living in a way that reflected God's standards, not out of obligation, but out of love and reverence. I examined my life, seeking areas where I needed to align more closely with God's righteousness. It was a call to integrity, to let my actions be a testimony of my faith.

The shoes of the gospel of peace were a reminder that I was to carry the message of Christ wherever I went. This was not just about evangelism; it was about living a life of peace and reconciliation. Every step I took needed to reflect the peace that Christ had brought into my life.

The shield of faith was essential in quenching the fiery darts of the enemy. Doubts, fears, and temptations would come, but with faith, I could extinguish them. Faith was not just belief; it was trust in God's promises, even when circumstances seemed contrary.

The helmet of salvation protected my mind. Salvation was more than a one-time event; it was an ongoing process of renewal and transformation. I needed to guard my thoughts, allowing God's salvation to shape my perspective and decisions.

Finally, the sword of the Spirit, which is the Word of God. This was my offensive weapon, the means by which I could counter the enemy's lies. Every time I declared God's Word, I was wielding a weapon of immense power.

I closed my journal, feeling a profound sense of readiness. The Armor of God was not just something to be admired; it was to be worn, every day, in every situation. As I prayed that night, I asked God to help me don this armor fully, to live in the strength and power He had provided.

The next morning, I woke up early, filled with a sense of anticipation. I knew that my faith journey was about to enter a new phase. At our weekly gathering, I shared my insights about the Armor of God with the group. Brother James nodded, his eyes shining with approval.

"You're absolutely right," he said. "The Armor of God is our protection and our weaponry. It's what enables us to stand firm against the forces of darkness. But remember, we must put it on daily. It's a conscious decision, a daily commitment."

We decided to dedicate the next few weeks to studying each piece of the armor in depth, understanding not just its biblical significance but how to apply it practically in our lives. Each meeting was a time of revelation and empowerment. We discussed, prayed, and shared testimonies of how the Armor of God was making a difference in our spiritual battles.

One evening, as we gathered around a table covered with Bibles and notebooks, Sister Maria shared a powerful testimony. "I've always struggled with anxiety," she admitted, her voice trembling slightly. "But since I've been consciously putting on the helmet of salvation, I've experienced a peace that I can't explain. It's like my mind is being protected from the attacks that used to overwhelm me."

Her words resonated with all of us. We were experiencing firsthand the truth of God's Word, seeing the transformation it brought into our lives. The Armor of God was not just a concept; it was a living reality, equipping us to face the challenges of each day.

As we continued our journey, I felt a deep sense of gratitude. We were not alone in this battle. We had each other, and more importantly, we had God. The path ahead was still fraught with challenges, but we were armed and ready. Together, we would stand firm, advancing the Kingdom of God, one step at a time.

Chapter 9: Living as a Chosen People

The battle is relentless, but so is the strength of those who follow Yahshua HaMashiach. Brother James's voice carried a deep resonance as he spoke about the ongoing struggle against spiritual forces. "The enemy never rests," he said. "He's always looking for a way to break in, to disrupt your prayer life, and to pull you away from the path of righteousness."

It was clear that spiritual warfare was not just about isolated incidents—it was a continuous battle that required vigilance, prayer, and a deep connection to God. Brother James urged us to stay rooted in the Word, to immerse ourselves in the Bible, and to trust in the promises of God. "All glory be to the Most High," he said, reminding us that no matter how intense the battle, God's power was greater.

"We came from the dust, and to the dust, we will return," he continued, "but while we are here, we must live in a way that honours God."

Spiritual Awakening 147

He spoke about the historical examples of great kings who fell because of their pride or wickedness. Pharaoh, Nebuchadnezzar, and others—all were brought low when they chose to defy God. "The Word of God is our guide," Brother James said. "Follow the path, and you will not be led astray."

As he shared his insights, I marvelled at how easily a brief conversation had turned into a full-fledged sermon. It was as if the Holy Spirit had taken control, transforming a simple meeting into a powerful moment of revelation.

"Wow, Brother James, thank you," I said, offering him a chance to catch his breath. He nodded, acknowledging that the Spirit was indeed at work.

"The spiritual battle is real," he continued, "and it's not just about avoiding sin—it's about embracing the light, choosing to walk in the Spirit, and standing firm in your faith." He explained that the key to overcoming spiritual attacks was to stay focused on God, to pray with intensity, and to seek His guidance in all things. "When you do God's work, the enemy will try to stop you," he said. "But that's when you know you're on the right track."

Brother James also mentioned the importance of community and fellowship. "We can't do this alone," he said. "Surround yourself with people who share your faith, who will support you and encourage you when the battle gets tough." He emphasized the need for spiritual discernment, to recognize when the enemy is trying to infiltrate and to respond with prayer and the Word of God.

Our conversation touched on the concept of spiritual training. Brother James explained that the trials we face are opportunities to grow stronger in our faith. "It's never really gonna fully stop," he said, referring to the spiritual attacks. "But you're in training, and you'll grow in strength as you keep on the path."

He encouraged us to take our spiritual growth seriously, to pray, fast, and study the Bible with a renewed sense of purpose. "Spiritual awakening is crucial," he said. "It's what allows you to see beyond the surface, to understand the deeper forces at play, and to respond with the right tools."

By the end of our conversation, I felt a sense of clarity and determination. Brother James's words were a powerful reminder that the journey of faith is not a straight line—it's filled with twists, turns, and unexpected challenges. But with Yahshua HaMashiach as our guide, and the Holy Spirit as our source of strength, there's no battle we can't overcome.

This chapter in my journey is about finding strength in spiritual battles, about learning to stand firm in the face of adversity, and about embracing the path that leads to righteousness.

It's a call to action, a reminder that we must stay vigilant and committed to the fight, knowing that with God on our side, victory is assured.

Brother James," I said, "tomorrow, I'm going to need those spiritual warfare prayers you mentioned." He nodded, a knowing look in his eyes. "At the end of this book, we'll include them for the readers," he replied. "Listen, when you're chosen and have a mission, the enemy is going to be against you. You'll face resistance, so you need to be prepared. I want to give you the tools that have helped me and prepare you for the battles ahead."

He emphasized the importance of community and mutual support among believers. "We must do our best to support one another," he said.

"There's power in the tongue, so we must be careful not to speak negative things into our lives. The words we use can either build us up or tear us down. Let's choose words that bring life and encouragement."

Before we continued, Brother James suggested we start the chapter with the Lord's Prayer, a foundational prayer for all believers. It was a reminder of the spiritual authority we have and the protection we can claim in Yahshua' name.

"Our Father, who art in heaven,

Hallowed be Thy name.

Thy kingdom come, Thy will be done

On earth as it is in heaven.

Give us this day our daily bread,

And forgive us our trespasses,

As we forgive those who trespass against us.

And lead us not into temptation,

But deliver us from evil.

Spiritual Awakening 147

For Thine is the kingdom, and the power, and the glory,

Forever and ever. Amen."

As we finished the prayer, Brother James continued, asking for divine protection for those involved in the mission. "Protect us from the evil eye or ear, and protect us all, covering us in the blood of Yahshua. Remove all hearts and minds that are evil from this table the Lord has prepared for us. Let no evil come near us."

The atmosphere was charged with a sense of spiritual urgency. We knew the battles ahead would be challenging, but with the right tools and the Lord's protection, we felt ready to face them. Brother James's emphasis on spiritual warfare prayers was a crucial part of this preparation. By arming ourselves with these prayers and the power of the Holy Spirit, we could withstand any attack and stay on the path God had set before us.

As we closed the chapter, I realized that this journey was about more than just overcoming spiritual warfare—it was about embracing the mission and purpose that God had given us. It was about being a light in a dark world and

Spiritual Awakening 147

using our words to bring hope and encouragement to others.

The road ahead might be fraught with challenges, but with faith, prayer, and the support of our spiritual community, we could face anything. And with the Lord's Prayer as our guiding light, we were reminded that we were never alone in this journey. No matter how fierce the battle, we had the ultimate protector on our side, guiding us toward victory. " Brother James began, his voice resonating with authority. "I sprinkle the blood of Yahshua over our homes—walls, ceilings, windows, and doors. Thank you, Father God, for this powerful testimony." The words carried a profound sense of spiritual strength, reinforcing the protective power of invoking the blood of Yahshua.

As Brother James prayed, I felt the weight of his words and the depth of his faith. It wasn't just a ritual—it was a declaration of divine protection, a barrier against the forces of evil that might seek to disrupt the work we were doing. "Right now," he continued, "I cover this work and inspiration in Yahshua's name. Let the sacred plans come to fruition as we plead the blood and block any unseen evil, any spying spirits, from this conversation and these reasoning."

Spiritual warfare was not a light matter. It required faith, vigilance, and a constant connection to God. Brother James understood this deeply, and his prayers reflected the seriousness of the battle. "Cover the reader and the writers," he said, his voice firm yet compassionate, "in Yahshua Yahshua's mighty name. Amen."

His prayer reminded us that the work of creating this book was more than just putting words on a page—it was a mission to spread light in a world filled with darkness. By invoking the blood of Yahshua, we acknowledged the ultimate source of our strength and protection. The blood represented the sacrifice of Christ, the ultimate act of love that opened the door to salvation.

Brother James's prayer was a shield against the spiritual attacks that could arise from sharing our testimonies. It was a call to fortify our homes, our minds, and our hearts against the enemy's schemes. By covering everything in the blood of Yahshua, we were asserting our faith and declaring that we belonged to the Lord.

As the prayer concluded, I felt a sense of calm and reassurance. The spiritual battles we faced might be intense, but we had the most powerful ally on our side. Brother James's words reminded me that the spiritual world is complex, but God's authority is absolute. No weapon formed against us could prosper when we stood under the banner of Yahshua.

This chapter was about more than just prayer—it was about creating a spiritual force field, a sanctuary where God's presence was palpable. It was about ensuring that the work we were doing was protected from any negative influences, and that the testimony we shared would reach those who needed it most.

The prayer also served as a reminder that our words carry power. By speaking life and invoking the blood of Yahshua, we could change the spiritual atmosphere, turning darkness into light. It was a call to be mindful of what we say, knowing that our words can either build up or tear down.

As we moved forward, I knew that the journey would require continuous prayer, faith, and spiritual discernment. Brother James's prayer was a guiding light, showing us how to navigate the challenges ahead while staying grounded in our faith. It was a reminder that, no matter what we faced, we were not alone. With the blood of Yahshua as our covering, we could stand strong against any attack and complete the mission God had given us.

Chapter 10: The Journey of Endurance

The journey of spiritual warfare is ongoing, a relentless battle that requires endurance and vigilance. Throughout my journey, I've come to understand that the struggles we face are not just physical or emotional, but deeply spiritual. The enemy is constantly seeking ways to disrupt, discourage, and divert us from the path that leads to God.

In this chapter, I reflect on the lessons learned, the challenges faced, and the victories gained. The reality of spiritual warfare is that it doesn't end; it's a continuous process of growth, learning, and resistance. Each day presents new opportunities to grow stronger in faith, and new challenges to overcome.

One of the key lessons I've learned is the importance of spiritual discipline. This means staying rooted in prayer, reading the Word of God, and maintaining a constant connection to the Holy Spirit. When we keep our spiritual disciplines strong, we're better equipped to withstand the attacks that come our way.

Another important aspect of spiritual warfare is community. Isolation is one of the enemy's most powerful tools. When we're alone, we're more vulnerable to doubt and temptation. But when we're connected to a community of believers, we find strength, support, and encouragement. This fellowship is essential for spiritual growth and resilience.

I've also realized that spiritual warfare requires a deep understanding of God's Word. The Bible is our ultimate weapon, filled with promises and truths that can help us overcome any challenge. When we face attacks, we must turn to scripture for guidance and strength. It is through the Word of God that we find the courage to stand firm.

This journey has taught me the importance of spiritual discernment. The enemy's tactics are often subtle, designed to confuse and mislead. We need to be aware of his schemes and stay alert to his attempts to infiltrate our thoughts and actions. Spiritual discernment allows us to recognize these tactics and respond with the power of the Holy Spirit.

As I reflect on the ongoing nature of spiritual warfare, I'm reminded of the ultimate victory we have in Christ. No matter how intense the battle, we know that Yahshua has already defeated the enemy. This knowledge gives us the confidence to face each day with hope and determination.

The journey continues, and each step brings new revelations and insights. It's a journey of growth, learning, and transformation. As we walk this path, we must stay focused on God, trusting in His guidance and strength. With faith as our foundation and the Holy Spirit as our guide, we can overcome any obstacle.

Spiritual warfare is not something to fear; it's an opportunity to grow stronger in faith and closer to God. As we continue this journey, let's remember that we are not alone. God is with us, guiding us through the battles, and leading us toward victory. May we stay faithful, stay strong, and continue to fight the good fight. The journey continues, but with God on our side, we have nothing to fear.

In the midst of spiritual warfare, it's easy to feel overwhelmed by the intensity of the battles we face. Yet, the journey of faith is not one we walk alone. God is our constant guide and source of strength, providing us with the tools and resources we need to persevere. This chapter is a reminder to stay strong in faith and continually seek guidance from God, even when the road ahead seems uncertain.

One of the most powerful ways to stay strong in faith is through prayer. When we pray, we connect directly with God, opening our hearts to His wisdom and allowing His Spirit to work within us. Prayer is our lifeline in times of trouble, our source of comfort when we're weary, and our means of communicating with the Almighty. By maintaining a consistent prayer life, we find the strength to face any challenge.

Another key to staying strong in faith is immersing ourselves in the Word of God. The Bible is more than a collection of ancient texts; it is a living source of truth that speaks to us in every situation. Through scripture, we learn about God's character, His promises, and His plans for our lives. By reading and meditating on the Bible, we can draw closer to God and gain the guidance we need to navigate the complexities of life.

Community is also vital in our spiritual journey. Surrounding ourselves with fellow believers creates a supportive environment where we can share our struggles, encourage one another, and grow together in faith. When we are part of a community, we are reminded that we are not alone in our battles. Others have faced similar challenges and found victory through faith in God.

It's important to remember that spiritual warfare is not a sign of failure; it's a natural part of the Christian journey. The enemy attacks those who pose a threat to his kingdom, and our commitment to God makes us targets. Yet, these attacks also reveal the strength and resilience of our faith. By staying strong and seeking guidance from God, we turn these challenges into opportunities for growth and transformation.

Spiritual Awakening 147

In times of spiritual warfare, we must also rely on the power of the Holy Spirit. The Spirit provides us with discernment, wisdom, and the ability to stand firm in the face of adversity. By yielding to the Spirit's guidance, we can overcome any obstacle and continue to walk the path of righteousness.

As we continue this journey, let us remember that God's grace is sufficient for us. His power is made perfect in our weakness, and He will never leave us or forsake us. By seeking His guidance, we can find the courage to persevere, no matter how challenging the road may be.

This chapter is a call to remain steadfast in faith, to seek God's guidance in all things, and to trust that He is leading us toward victory. The journey of faith is ongoing, but with God as our guide, we have nothing to fear. Let us encourage one another, support one another, and continue to seek the guidance of the Lord as we walk this path together.

Spiritual Awakening 147

125
Reflections on the Ongoing Nature of Spiritual Warfare

Spiritual warfare is a journey, and every step presents opportunities for growth and transformation. As we continue this path, we must keep in mind that the enemy seeks to undermine our faith and derail our progress. Yet, through these challenges, we find the seeds of growth that, when nurtured, lead to a deeper, more resilient spirituality.

Spiritual growth is not a destination but an ongoing process. It requires us to continually seek God, engage with His Word, and develop our relationship with Him. In the crucible of spiritual warfare, our character is tested, and our faith is refined. The struggles we face become a catalyst for transformation, pushing us to grow stronger, wiser, and more reliant on God's grace.

One of the keys to spiritual growth is embracing transformation, even when it's uncomfortable. Transformation involves shedding old habits, beliefs, and behaviours that no longer align with God's will. It means allowing God to shape us into the people He has called us to be, even if that process requires sacrifice and surrender.

Throughout this journey, we must remain open to the guidance of the Holy Spirit. The Spirit is our teacher, comforter, and guide, helping us navigate the complexities of spiritual warfare. By staying attuned to the Spirit's leading, we can avoid the enemy's traps and make choices that reflect our commitment to God.

Spiritual growth also involves learning from others who have walked this path before us. Surrounding ourselves with mentors, spiritual leaders, and a supportive faith community provides us with the wisdom and encouragement we need to keep moving forward. These relationships offer valuable insights and accountability, ensuring that we stay on track and continue to grow.

As we reflect on the importance of spiritual growth and transformation, we must remember that God is patient with us. He understands our struggles and is always ready to help us when we stumble. Our journey is not about achieving

Spiritual Awakening 147

perfection; it's about striving to become more like Christ, one step at a time.

Final thoughts on spiritual growth and transformation: The journey is challenging, but it's also deeply rewarding. As we continue to grow in faith, we find that each trial brings us closer to God. Our experiences, though sometimes difficult, become the foundation for a stronger, more resilient faith.

Spiritual transformation is not a linear process; it's filled with ups and downs, victories and setbacks. But through it all, we can trust that God is at work in our lives, moulding us into the people He has destined us to be. By staying focused on Him, seeking His guidance, and embracing the changes He brings, we will find that our journey leads us to places of profound growth and transformation.

Ultimately, spiritual growth is about becoming the best version of ourselves, the version that God has envisioned from the beginning. It's about shedding the old and embracing the new, walking in the light of God's truth, and allowing His love to transform us from the inside out. As we continue this journey, let us

Spiritual Awakening 147

hold fast to our faith, encourage one another, and trust that God is with us every step of the way.

Following and keeping the commandments of the Most High has timeless significance, transcending generations and contexts. Here's why adherence to these commandments was essential in the past:

Spiritual Guidance: The commandments provided clear moral and ethical directives, helping individuals align their lives with divine will and spiritual principles.

Social Harmony: By adhering to these commandments, communities could foster peace, justice, and cooperation. They established a shared framework for right and wrong, which was crucial for maintaining order and harmony.

Covenant Relationship: For many, especially in the Judeo-Christian tradition, keeping the commandments was a way to honor the covenant with God. It was an expression of faithfulness and commitment to a sacred relationship.

Personal Integrity: Following the commandments helped individuals cultivate virtues such as honesty, kindness, and humility. This personal integrity was not only spiritually fulfilling but also beneficial in their daily interactions.

Divine Protection and Blessings: Many believed that adherence to the commandments would lead to divine protection and blessings. This included both material well-being and spiritual rewards.

Community Identity: The commandments often served as a foundational element of community identity, distinguishing the followers of the Most High from others and uniting them through shared beliefs and practices.

Moral Education: They provided a basis for teaching and transmitting values across generations, ensuring that children and newcomers to the faith understood and adhered to these important principles.

Chapter 11: Spiritual Warfare Prayers

Spiritual warfare is a constant battle that requires the full armour of God. Prayer is one of the most powerful weapons we have to combat the enemy's attacks. This chapter provides a collection of spiritual warfare prayers to help you stay strong, protected, and guided by the Holy Spirit. Use these prayers to fortify your spiritual defences, seek God's protection, and declare His victory over any forces that seek to harm you.

Prayer for Divine Protection

Heavenly Father, I come before You in the name of Yahshua, asking for Your divine protection. Cover me with Your precious blood, and surround me with Your angels. Keep me safe from all harm and spiritual attacks. Let no weapon formed against me prosper, and may Your presence be my shield. I trust in Your promise to never leave me nor forsake me. In Yahshua' name, I pray. Amen.

Spiritual Awakening 147

Prayer for Strength and Courage

Lord, I seek Your strength and courage as I face the battles ahead. I know that spiritual warfare can be intense, but I trust in Your power. Fill me with Your Holy Spirit, and grant me the courage to stand firm in my faith. Help me to overcome fear and doubt, and guide me through the challenges that come my way. I declare that I am victorious in Yahshua' name. Amen.

Prayer for Discernment

Father, I ask for the gift of discernment to recognize the tactics of the enemy. Give me the wisdom to know what is from You and what is not. Help me to discern truth from deception, and grant me the ability to make wise choices. May Your Word be a lamp to my feet and a light to my path. I trust in Your guidance, and I thank You for Your constant presence. In Yahshua' name, I pray. Amen.

Prayer for Breaking Strongholds

Lord Yahshua, I come against any strongholds in my life that are keeping me from experiencing Your fullness. I break every chain of addiction, every pattern of sin, and every spirit of oppression in Your mighty name. I declare that I am free from the enemy's grip, and I ask for Your healing touch to restore me completely. Thank You for Your power and for the freedom I have in You. Amen.

Prayer for Spiritual Armor

Father, I put on the whole armor of God, as described in Ephesians 6:10-18. I wear the belt of truth, the breastplate of righteousness, and the shoes of the gospel of peace. I take up the shield of faith to extinguish the fiery darts of the enemy, and I wear the helmet of salvation. I hold the sword of the Spirit, which is the Word of God, and I stand firm in Your power. Equip me for battle, and help me to remain steadfast. In Yahshua' name, I pray. Amen.

133
Prayer for Victory over the Enemy

Lord, I declare victory over the enemy in Your name. I know that You have already defeated Satan and his forces, and I claim that victory for myself and my loved ones. Help me to walk in Your truth and to resist the enemy's lies. I ask for Your protection over my family, my home, and my workplace. May Your light shine through me, and may I be a witness to Your power. In Yahshua' name, I pray. Amen.

Guidance

These spiritual warfare prayers are designed to empower you in your journey of faith. Use them as a foundation for your own prayers, and remember that the power of prayer comes from your relationship with God. Stay connected to Him, and He will guide you through every battle. The enemy may be relentless, but with God on your side, you are unstoppable. Keep praying, keep trusting, and keep fighting the good fight.

Spiritual warfare requires constant vigilance and reliance on God's strength. As we continue to explore spiritual warfare prayers, remember that these prayers are more than words—they

Spiritual Awakening 147

are expressions of faith, declarations of truth, and calls for divine intervention. Use these prayers to strengthen your relationship with God and fortify your defences against spiritual attacks.

Prayer for Clarity and Focus

Heavenly Father, I ask for clarity and focus as I navigate the challenges of spiritual warfare. Remove any confusion, doubt, or distractions that could lead me astray. Help me to stay focused on You and Your will for my life. I pray for a clear mind and a steadfast heart, ready to face whatever comes my way. Guide me with Your Spirit, and let Your truth be my anchor. In Yahshua' name, I pray. Amen.

Prayer for Protection Against Spiritual Oppression

Lord, I ask for Your protection against any form of spiritual oppression. I come against any evil forces that seek to disrupt my peace and joy. Cover me with Your blood, and let no harmful spirit gain access to my heart or mind. I rebuke all forms of darkness and claim Your light over my life. Thank You for being my refuge and fortress. In Yahshua' name, I pray. Amen.

Prayer for Guidance and Wisdom

Father, I seek Your guidance and wisdom in every decision I make. Help me to discern Your voice amid the noise and to choose the path that aligns with Your will. Give me the wisdom to know when to act and when to wait, and grant me the patience to trust in Your timing. May I find peace in Your guidance and strength in Your presence. In Yahshua' name, I pray. Amen.

Prayer for Family Protection

Lord, I lift up my family to You, asking for Your protection and guidance. Keep them safe from all harm and spiritual attacks. Guard their hearts and minds, and fill our home with Your peace and love. I pray that we would be united in faith and that our family would be a source of light in a dark world. May Your blessings be upon us, and may we always find refuge in You. In Yahshua' name, I pray. Amen.

Prayer for Deliverance and Healing

Heavenly Father, I ask for deliverance from any spiritual bondage that may be holding me back. Break every chain, every curse, and every form of oppression in the mighty name of Yahshua. I pray for complete healing and restoration, both physically and spiritually. Fill me with Your healing touch, and renew my spirit with Your love. Thank You for the freedom I have in You. In Yahshua' name, I pray. Amen.

These spiritual warfare prayers are designed to help you stay strong in faith and seek God's guidance in every situation. Remember, spiritual warfare is a continuous battle, but with God on your side, you have the ultimate source of strength and protection. Use these prayers as a foundation for your daily devotion and as a reminder that you are never alone in this journey.

137

Stay vigilant, keep praying, and trust that God will lead you through every challenge. The enemy may be relentless, but with these prayers and God's guidance, you can overcome any obstacle and walk in victory. Keep your faith strong, and remember that you are a child of God, protected and empowered by His Spirit.

Chapter 12: Praise and Declaring God's Glory

The journey through spiritual warfare has taught me many things, but the most powerful lesson is the importance of praise and declaring God's glory. When we lift our voices in praise, we acknowledge God's sovereignty over all things. We affirm His power, His love, and His unending mercy. In this final chapter, I invite you to join me in a celebration of God's glory, focusing on the strength we gain through worship and the transformation that comes from living in His light. Praise is more than just singing songs or reciting verses; it's a declaration of our faith, a reminder that no matter what we face, God is with us. When we praise, we shift our focus from our struggles to His greatness. We invite His presence into our lives, allowing His Spirit to work in and through us. Praise is both a weapon against spiritual warfare and a source of joy and renewal.

Spiritual Awakening 147

The Bible is filled with examples of praise and worship, from the Psalms to the early church. King David, known for his heart of worship, wrote many Psalms that express deep devotion and adoration for God. His songs of praise became a source of strength during times of trial and adversity. "I will bless the Lord at all times; His praise shall continually be in my mouth," he wrote **(Psalm 34:1).** This attitude of constant praise is what sustains us in our journey of faith. As we declare God's glory, we also acknowledge His role in our lives. We recognize that every blessing, every moment of grace, comes from Him. By praising Him, we align our hearts with His purpose and open ourselves to His transformative power. Praise is an act of surrender, a way of saying, "God, I trust You, even when I don't understand."

In my own journey, I've found that praise has a way of breaking through the darkness. When I felt overwhelmed by spiritual warfare, I turned to praise as a source of strength. Whether through singing, prayer, or simply speaking words of gratitude, I discovered that praising God brought a sense of peace and clarity. It reminded me that no matter how intense the battle, God's presence was stronger.

Declaring God's glory is also about sharing our testimonies, telling others about the incredible things He's done in our lives. When we share our stories of faith, we inspire others to seek Him and to trust in His goodness. Our testimonies become a powerful witness, showing that God is real, active, and at work in the world.

As we conclude this book, I encourage you to make praise a regular part of your life. Whether in times of joy or times of struggle, let praise be your response. Declare God's glory in everything you do, and let your life be a testament to His greatness. When you face challenges, remember to praise Him, for He is always with you.

In closing, I want to thank you for joining me on this journey through spiritual warfare. It's not always easy, but with God on our side, we are never alone. Keep praising, keep declaring God's glory, and keep trusting that He is guiding you every step of the way.

Spiritual Awakening 147

With faith and obedience may this final chapter be a reminder that praise is the key to victory, and that through praise, we find the strength to continue our journey of faith. God bless you, and may His glory shine brightly in your life.

The Royal Line of Judah: The Lineage of the Messiah

From the ancient promises of God to the fulfilment in Jesus Christ, known as Yahshua, the story of the Messiah's lineage is a testament to divine sovereignty and faithfulness. The journey begins with Abraham and culminates in the birth of Jesus, our Lord and Saviour, tracing a path through the tribe of Judah and the royal line of David. This chapter explores the lineage of the Messiah and highlights the significance of each key figure in this sacred ancestry.

The Covenant with Abraham

God's plan for the redemption of humanity began with a covenant with Abraham. God promised Abraham that through his descendants, all nations of the earth would be blessed **(Genesis 12:3)**. This promise set the stage for the unfolding of God's redemptive plan.

Isaac and Jacob: The Promises Continued

Isaac, the promised son of Abraham, inherited the blessings and covenant promises **(Genesis 17:19)**. Isaac's son, Jacob, who was later named Israel, fathered twelve sons who became the patriarchs of the twelve tribes of Israel **(Genesis 28:14)**. Among these sons was Judah, from whom the royal line would emerge.

Judah: The Tribe of Kingship

Judah, the fourth son of Jacob and Leah, was chosen for a special role. Despite not being the firstborn, Judah received the blessing of leadership and kingship. Jacob's prophetic blessing upon Judah declared, "The scepter will not depart from Judah, nor the ruler's staff from between his feet, until he to whom it belongs shall come and the obedience of the nations shall be his" **(Genesis 49:10).** This prophecy foretold that the Messiah would come from Judah's lineage.

Perez to David: Establishing the Royal Line

Judah's lineage continued through his son Perez, who was born to Tamar (Genesis 38:29). The line of Perez progressed through generations, including **Hezron, Ram, Amminadab, Nahshon, Salmon, Boaz, Obed, and Jesse (Ruth 4:18-22). Jesse's son, David,** became the most significant figure in this lineage.

David, the youngest son of Jesse, was anointed by the prophet Samuel as the king of Israel **(1 Samuel 16:12-13)**. God made a covenant with David, promising that his throne would be established forever and that his lineage would produce the eternal king **(2 Samuel 7:12-16)**. This covenant solidified the Messianic promise within the line of David.

Solomon and the Continuation of the Royal Line

David's son, Solomon, succeeded him as king and built the temple in Jerusalem **(1 Kings 1:39)**. Solomon's wisdom and reign further established the prominence of David's line. Despite the subsequent division of the kingdom

Spiritual Awakening 147

and the eventual exile of the Israelites, the promise of an eternal king from David's lineage remained steadfast.

The Fulfilment in Yahshua (Jesus Christ)

Centuries later, the promises and prophecies found their fulfilment in Jesus Christ, known as Yahshua. The New Testament provides genealogies that trace Jesus' lineage back to David, affirming His rightful place in the royal line of Judah.

Matthew's Genealogy: The Gospel of Matthew traces Jesus' legal lineage through Joseph, His adoptive father, showing His legal right to David's throne **(Matthew 1:1-16)**. This genealogy emphasizes Jesus' role as the promised King of the Jews.

Luke's Genealogy: The Gospel of Luke provides a genealogy that many scholars believe traces Jesus' biological lineage through Mary, affirming His bloodline descent from David **(Luke 3:23-38)**. This genealogy highlights Jesus' humanity and fulfilment of the Davidic covenant.

In the book of Revelation, Jesus is referred to as the "Lion of the tribe of Judah, the Root of David" **(Revelation 5:5),** confirming His identity as the Messiah. His life, death, and resurrection fulfil the ancient promises and establish Him as the anointed Saviour of the world.

The Eternal Legacy of Yahshua

The lineage of Yahshua, our Lord and Savior, is not just a historical account but a divine narrative woven through generations, fulfilling promises and prophecies with meticulous precision. From the covenant with Abraham, through the royal line of David, and culminating in the birth of Jesus Christ, the thread of God's plan for redemption is unmistakable.

The Faithfulness of God

The journey through the lineage of the Messiah reveals the unwavering faithfulness of God. Despite human failings and the passage of centuries, God's promises remained steadfast. He chose individuals and orchestrated events to bring about His ultimate purpose—the salvation of humanity through Yahshua.

The Role of Judah and David

The tribe of Judah was set apart for kingship, and through David, God established an eternal covenant. David's line, though marked by triumphs and tribulations, carried the seed of the Messiah. The significance of this lineage cannot be overstated, as it underscores the prophetic and royal heritage of Jesus Christ.

The Fulfilment in Yahshua

In Yahshua, the prophecies and promises converge. His birth in Bethlehem, His ministry, His sacrificial death, and His victorious resurrection all attest to His identity as the promised Messiah. The genealogies in Matthew and Luke highlight His rightful place in the line of David, affirming Him as the Lion of the tribe of Judah and the Root of David.

The Impact of the Messiah

Yahshua's life and mission transformed the course of history. He brought the message of God's kingdom, demonstrated love and compassion, and offered Himself as the ultimate sacrifice for sin. Through His resurrection, He conquered death, offering eternal life to all who believe in Him.

Our Response to the Messiah

Understanding the lineage and mission of Yahshua invites us to respond in faith. He is not just a historical figure but the living Savior who calls each of us to follow Him. His royal lineage and divine mission compel us to recognize His authority and embrace the salvation He offers.

The Eternal Kingdom

The promise of an eternal kingdom, rooted in the line of David and fulfilled in Yahshua, gives us hope for the future. As believers, we are part of this kingdom, awaiting the return of our King who will reign forever in justice and peace.

Final Reflection

The story of Yahshua's lineage is a profound testament to God's sovereignty, faithfulness, and love. It bridges the Old and New Testaments, connecting ancient prophecies with their fulfilment in Christ. As we reflect on this divine narrative, we are reminded of our place in God's redemptive plan and the eternal hope we have in Yahshua, our Lord.

May this understanding deepen our faith, inspire our worship, and encourage us to live in the light of His coming kingdom. For in Yahshua, the Lion of the tribe of Judah and the Root of David, we find our eternal King and the source of our salvation.

**All praises to the Most High Yahuah, God Almighty.
All glory be to the Son, Yahshua HaMashiach,
Saviour of Israel, the Messiah, the Chosen One.**

Notes for Readers

Thank you for taking the time to read Spiritual Warfare: A Journey of Faith. This book is designed to inspire, encourage, and guide you on your own spiritual journey. To further assist you in your walk of faith, we've compiled some additional resources and suggestions for further reading. We also offer contact information for support groups and faith-based communities that can provide you with ongoing support and encouragement.

Additional Resources for Spiritual Growth and Understanding

The Bible: The ultimate source for spiritual wisdom and guidance. Consider reading the Gospels, Psalms, and the Book of Proverbs for encouragement and insight.

Prayer and Meditation Guides: Look for resources that offer structured prayers and meditations to deepen your spiritual connection.

Online Sermons and Podcasts: Many churches and religious organizations offer online sermons and podcasts that can provide spiritual guidance and inspiration.

Suggestions for Further Reading

"The Screw tape Letters" by C.S. Lewis: An insightful exploration of spiritual warfare from the perspective of a senior demon advising a junior demon on how to tempt a human soul.

"Spiritual Warfare: The Invisible Invasion" by Thomas R. Horn: A comprehensive guide to understanding spiritual warfare and how it affects our daily lives.

"The Spiritual Man" by Watchman Nee: A detailed examination of the human spirit and the importance of living a spiritually-focused life.

Contact Information for Support Groups and Faith-Based Communities

Local Churches: Find a church community in your area where you can connect with others who share your faith. Look for churches that offer Bible studies, prayer groups, and fellowship activities.

Spiritual Awakening 147

Online Faith-Based Communities: Websites like Faith Gateway and Cross walk provide articles, devotionals, and forums for spiritual growth and discussion.

Christian Counselling Services: If you're dealing with spiritual struggles, consider reaching out to a Christian counsellor or therapist who can offer guidance and support. Look for counsellors who are licensed and have experience in faith-based counselling.

Staying Connected

We hope this book has been a source of encouragement for you. If you'd like to connect with us or share your own experiences, please reach out through our website or social media platforms. We value your feedback and look forward to hearing from you.

Remember, the journey of faith is ongoing, and you're not alone. Seek out those who can support and uplift you as you continue to grow spiritually. May this book be a stepping stone to a deeper relationship with God and a stronger understanding of spiritual warfare

Acknowledgments

Completing Spiritual Warfare: A Journey of Faith has been a profound experience, and I could not have done it without the invaluable contributions and support of many individuals and groups. This section is dedicated to expressing my gratitude to those who played a significant role in the creation of this book.

Contributing Influences

I want to extend my deepest thanks to Brother James, whose testimony and spiritual insights inspired much of this book. His journey of faith and dedication to spreading God's word have been a guiding light throughout the writing process.

A special thanks to the members of my church community for their constant encouragement, prayer, and fellowship. Their support has been instrumental in keeping me focused and motivated during the most challenging moments.

I also want to recognize the many mentors, pastors, and spiritual leaders who have provided guidance and wisdom.

Spiritual Awakening 147- James Stephenson

LoveGodNow Ministry - John Livingston

Their teachings have shaped my understanding of spiritual warfare and the importance of walking in the Spirit.

Gratitude for Spiritual Guidance

My heartfelt gratitude goes to God, who is the source of all truth and wisdom. His presence has been my anchor and my strength, providing me with the inspiration and courage to write about these important topics. I am thankful for the Holy Spirit's guidance, which has led me through the ups and downs of this journey.

I also want to express my appreciation to my family and friends, who have stood by me through thick and thin. Their love and encouragement have been a constant reminder that I am not alone in this journey.

Closing Thoughts

Spiritual Awakening 147

Thank you to everyone who has contributed to this book, whether through direct input, prayer, or simply by being there when I needed support. Your impact has been immeasurable, and I am deeply grateful for your presence in my life.

To my readers, thank you for taking the time to explore Spiritual Warfare: A Journey of Faith. I hope it brings you clarity, strength, and inspiration as you navigate your own spiritual journey. Remember, you are not alone, and there are many who walk this path with you. May God bless you and guide you always

About the Author

Brother James is a man of profound faith, a spiritual warrior whose journey has been marked by extraordinary experiences and a deep commitment to serving God. Raised in Brixton, a vibrant yet challenging part of London, Brother James has lived through some of life's toughest trials. His story is one of transformation, redemption, and unwavering faith in the face of spiritual warfare.

Throughout his early years, Brother James navigated the complexities of urban life, often finding himself at odds with the environment around him. He experienced violence, temptation, and the lure of the streets. Despite these challenges, he always felt a divine presence guiding him, even when he didn't fully understand it. It wasn't until a life-changing encounter with God that he realized he had a higher purpose.

Brother James's spiritual journey took a dramatic turn when he began to experience intense spiritual warfare. These battles, both seen and unseen, challenged him to his core, forcing him to seek a deeper connection with God. Through prayer, fasting, and a renewed dedication to reading the Bible, he found the strength to overcome the forces that sought to pull him away from his faith.

His testimony is one of miraculous interventions and moments of divine protection. From surviving violent attacks to experiencing spiritual revelations, Brother James has witnessed God's hand at work in his life. These experiences have fuelled his passion for sharing his story and helping others navigate their own spiritual battles.

As an advocate for spiritual growth and transformation, Brother James is committed to equipping others with the knowledge and tools they need to combat spiritual warfare. He believes in the power of community and the importance of supporting one another through the journey of faith. His teachings emphasize the significance of prayer, the study of God's Word, and the importance of maintaining a strong spiritual connection.

Brother James's autobiography and testimonial book is a reflection of his life, a journey from darkness to light, from struggle to victory. It's a testament to the enduring power of faith and the unyielding grace of God. Through his story, Brother James aims to inspire others to embrace their own spiritual awakening and to find strength in the Lord.

In addition to his work in spiritual ministry, Brother James is dedicated to mentoring and guiding those who seek a deeper understanding of spiritual warfare. He encourages readers to stay vigilant, to speak words of life, and to keep their focus on Yahshua. His message is clear: with God on your side, no battle is too great, and every struggle can be overcome.

As you read Brother James's story, may you find inspiration, encouragement, and the motivation to walk in your own spiritual journey with confidence. This book is a reminder that we are all chosen for a purpose, and with faith, we can achieve great things for the glory of God.

The Author's Spiritual Journey and Personal Experiences

Brother James's spiritual journey is a powerful testament to the transformative impact of faith and the relentless pursuit of God's purpose. Growing up in Brixton, he was exposed to the harsh realities of street life, where violence, crime, and temptation were all too common. Yet even in the darkest moments, he felt a subtle pull toward something greater—an unseen force guiding him through the chaos.

His early experiences were filled with challenges that tested his resolve and faith.

From a young age, Brother James found himself at the crossroads of two opposing paths: one leading deeper into the streets, and the other toward spiritual awakening. It wasn't always easy to choose the latter, but a series of events made it clear that his destiny was not tied to the streets but to a higher calling.

One such turning point was a violent attack that he miraculously survived. This encounter, which could have ended his life, instead became a catalyst for his spiritual transformation. Brother James knew he had been saved for a reason, and it was then that he began to seek a deeper connection with God. He realized that spiritual warfare was real and that he needed to arm himself with prayer, faith, and the Word of God to withstand the enemy's assaults.

Throughout his journey, Brother James experienced moments of divine intervention that solidified his faith. There were times when he felt the presence of the Lord in a tangible way, lifting him out of pain and despair. These moments were not just isolated incidents but signs of a loving God who was actively involved in his life. From dreams that provided guidance to miraculous encounters that saved him from harm, Brother James learned to trust in God's timing and direction.

As he grew in his spiritual journey, Brother James became passionate about sharing his testimony with others. He understood that his experiences, though unique, could inspire and encourage those facing similar struggles. His journey from darkness to light, from chaos to spiritual clarity, became a beacon for others seeking hope and redemption.

Brother James's personal experiences also taught him the importance of community and fellowship. He found strength in connecting with other believers who supported him through prayer and spiritual guidance. This sense of community became a cornerstone of his journey, reminding him that spiritual warfare is not a battle to be fought alone.

In his pursuit of spiritual growth, Brother James embraced practices that helped him stay connected to God. Prayer became a central part of his life, a constant source of strength and guidance. He also devoted himself to studying the Bible, seeking wisdom and insight from its teachings. Through fasting and meditation, he deepened his relationship with God and learned to discern the enemy's tactics.

Brother James's personal experiences are a testament to the power of faith and the enduring grace of God. His journey serves as a reminder that even in the midst of spiritual warfare, there is hope, there is light, and there is a path to victory. As he continues to share his story, Brother James invites others to join him in this journey of faith, trusting that with God on their side, no battle is too great to overcome.

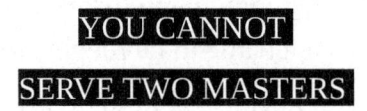

YOU CANNOT SERVE TWO MASTERS

THANK YOU FOR READING!

Printed in Great Britain
by Amazon